A CONCISE
ENGLISH-CHINESE
DICTIONARY

by

E. M. CHANG, PH. B.

Formerly Professor of Literature
Central University, Nanking

and

SHIRLEY MAXWELL

THE MARCEL  RODD CO.

1944

Published and printed in the U.S. by
THE MARCEL RODD COMPANY
1656 North Cherokee Avenue
Hollywood 28, California

CONTENTS

How to Use This Dictionary 7

The Four Tones 13

The Wade System of Transliteration 15

Text 19

Appendix 177

The Chinese Radicals 179

Table of Chinese Classifiers 185

Chinese Numerals 187

Periods of Chinese History 189

The Provinces of China 190

INTRODUCTION

HOW TO USE THIS DICTIONARY

This is not a pretentious book. It is not a bulky book. But it should prove useful and serviceable for the growing number of people who are studying the Chinese language seriously and who are handicapped by the absence of an adequate English-Chinese dictionary. There is no comparable dictionary on the market today. Those published in China are for the use of Chinese students who are studying the English language and are obviously not suited for Americans, Britishers, and others, who wish to have a working knowledge of the Chinese language.

The number of such people grew very rapidly all over the world, and more especially in the United States, as a result of the war. Whether for military reasons, or for purposes of commerce and diplomacy, China, in a very brief period became acknowledged as a country with which the English-speaking world should grow increasingly intimate, and a study of her language became widespread.

There are still many people who are misinformed on the subject of the dialects in China. The fact is that there are no more dialects in China than in any other country, and when one considers the size and extent of its territory, the surprising thing is that there are so few. However, even these dialects are all based on an identical written language which happens to be differently pronounced in different parts of the country. And there is only one pronunciation that is actually used in the greater part of China and this is now being officially enforced everywhere. This pronunciation is the so-called "Mandarin dialect" or, better still, *kuo yü*, the spoken Chinese National Language. It is this pronunciation which is used in this dictionary.

7

The student will find that there are four columns on each page. The first column includes about 4000 of the commonest words in the English language. There is nothing arbitrary in their choice — on the contrary, their selection was a matter of extreme care and individual consideration. It is not necessary to explain here with any detail the many elements that entered into their choice: suffice it to say that "greatest use" was the foundation for their choice, and that Chinese usage just as much as English was equally considered as each individual choice of a word was made. Briefly, too, we should state here that the nature of the Chinese language itself dictated the simplification of the choice of English words, there being no necessity for plural forms, adverbs, participles, etc.; and where, in English, an identical idea has its two forms for its verbal and nominative meanings (e.g. wound, *noun;* to wound, *verb*) only the English noun was needed as in Chinese the one word according to its manner of use expresses both noun and verb. Thus, the fact that Chinese is a language of ideas and not of parts of speech necessarily simplified, or at least shortened the list of English words called for. Were the list used here to be resolved into adverbs, adjectives, etc., in the manner of a dictionary of a European language our English word list would have easily reached to twice, or more than twice its present length.

The above bears restatement: —

Chinese nouns have no genitive and dative forms, and no plural. Thus, once you learn a word you know it. In Chinese, you do not have to contend with masculine, feminine, and neuter genders, as in other languages, nor with past and future tenses of verbs. Finally, the verbal and nominative "forms" of words which have both in English are identical.

However, you must realize that a simple word can radically change the meaning of a sentence by the position in which it is used. This peculiarity of the sentence structure is the basis of the spoken and written language. The same word can be used as a noun, an adjective, an adverb, or a verb. Its function, and therefore its precise meaning, depends on its position in the sentence in relation to the other words.

The student should learn how to indicate gender or sex. In English we speak of a she-cat; the Chinese always use this method to indicate gender or sex. Man, in English, is a masculine noun; in Chinese a woman is a lady-man. A dog is spoken of as a man-dog or a lady-dog. A noun has in itself no gender. The words man and lady must be prefixed to it if a gender is to be indicated.

Chinese words are always singular. However, plurality is suggested by the use of plural words, such as "mên"; thus "Hai tzu" means "child" and "hai tzu mên," "children."

Past and future are indicated by placing words referring to past and future before or after the verb. "The man walks" is in the present tense. To make it indicate future tense a Chinese would say "The man tomorrow

8

walks," or "The man next week walks," meaning the man will walk at the time indicated. The past tense is indicated by such words as: *liao* (to finish) and *kuo* (to pass), placed immediately after the verb.

A brief reference should be made to Chinese classifiers. In English we speak of pieces of sugar, head of cattle, loaves of bread, etc. The Chinese speak of one person-gentleman (meaning a gentleman), one tube-pen (meaning a pen), one seat-clock (meaning a clock) and one slice-visiting card (meaning a visiting card). The most common classifier is the Chinese word *ko*. It means piece: one piece-match, one piece-man, etc.

In the second column the compilers have listed the most exact Chinese equivalents in their written form. These characters have nothing to do with the dialects. They constitute the standard Chinese written language in universal use not only in China, but in the neighboring countries as well (Japan, Korea, Indo-China, etc.)

This written language has been in existence for more than 3000 years. But the form of its writing has naturally evolved through the centuries. The form which is used in the second column is of course the one in use in China today. This has been in use for at least fifteen hundred years.

Students will already be familiar with the fact that there are "three different Chinese languages" — the classical, the written, and the spoken. In this present volume the classical language has been by-passed completely, and the choice of the Chinese words has been made exclusively on the basis of written and spoken modern Chinese. There is a substantial difference between these two. In the choice of Chinese words for our second column the tendency was to favor written Chinese. However, this was done only when a "spoken" Chinese word seemed, of itself, inadequate. Frequently, in such instances, more than one translation is given. But the guiding light in this regard was an effort to find exact Chinese words which are good "written" Chinese and at the same time perfectly acceptable for "spoken" Chinese. Briefly, a real and sustained effort was made to compile a dictionary capable of filling a dual role.

The third column gives the pronunciation, so far as any "anglicised" form is able to give it, of the spoken National Language known in Chinese as the *kuo yii*. No attempt is made to give the pronunciation according to the different "dialects." That is not necessary if the *kuo yii* pronunciation is the standard pronunciation. A few words are, however, helpful in explaining this romanisation, or "anglicised" third column.

We must bear in mind that the Chinese language is infinitely richer in the production of single sounds than English or, for that matter, any other language where the words are constructed out of syllables. The reason is simple. In Chinese, which is a monosyllabic language, each word is represented by a single sound. That sound is, furthermore, not spelt out through an alphabet. It is purely arbitrary, and the same sound may therefore be given to a number of words written differently from one

9

another and having entirely different meanings. The student must learn to pronounce the words, not by any such mechanical device as an alphabet, but by ear, or by memorizing them, or by a recognition of the way in which they are written.

Further, in order to produce as many single sounds as possible, the Chinese have recourse to the tones. There are four for all practical purposes, which means, theoretically, that there are four times more sounds, or words, than the number of single sounds. And so our compilers' third column is merely an attempt, in so far as the alphabet of the English language permits, to reproduce the Chinese pronunciation of the second column by a simple and consistent rendering, complete with tone numbers. It is, so to say, "ready for use" independently of the fourth column, in which the famous and established, but obscure and often clumsy "Wade System" of transliteration is given.

That it can never be an *exact* reproduction should be clear. But it is believed that this third column is an improvement on the fourth column.

This fourth column is the pronunciation according to the Wade system. Sir Thomas Wade, in those early days of the 19th century, devised a system which proved to be both helpful and complete and which, by dint of usage and the passage of time, came to be recognized as more or less the standard form. A chart of the Wade system is included in this volume and a study of it will quickly reveal why so many objections have been raised to it.

The reason why it is included here is that it is so widely used, and indeed all new books on the Chinese language are obliged to include it if only to remain "in step" with the other texts which have previously appeared. Hence the self-perpetuation of the Wade system. People have become accustomed to the Wade form of spelling. It is given as a convenient reference and as a basis for improvement by the students themselves. Students are at liberty, in fact, to spell out the pronunciation of Chinese words in whatever way they prefer, so long as their own romanization conveys the most perfect pronunciation to *them*. Needless to say, no "column" in any dictionary can take the place, or completely serve the purpose of having one's ear accustomed to hearing the language spoken by Chinese. This is particularly true regarding the tones, to which a special section is devoted in this volume.

A last word. Once the difficulties of pronunciation are overcome, the Chinese language is not a difficult one to the average student. It is particularly suited for the adult because there is no need for him to remember the inflections, conjugations, genders, cases, etc., which make the study of any foreign language so boring and tiresome. The Chinese language has none of these encumbrances. The English language has evolved, and continues to evolve, in the direction of Chinese because we all realize how simple it has become as compared with German, which is originally from the same origins. That is why Otto Jespersen, one of the leading philologists of the day, has said that Chinese is perhaps the most highly developed language and that all languages have a tendency to develop towards the structure of Chinese. The study of Chinese may truthfully be said to be more interesting and certainly much easier than the study of most European languages. Both the authors and the publishers believe that this contribution toward a simplification of the student's labors will be invaluable.

The Four Tones

The four tones of the Mandarin dialect present a definite problem to the English speaking student of Chinese. Perhaps the clearest way of understanding these tones is to see a visual graph or picture of their relative sound value.

The first tone is called P'ing or even tone. This tone is high in pitch and may easily be prolonged without a break in the voice.

The second tone is Shang or rising tone. It rises from a lower to a higher level.

The third is Ch'u, departing tone. This tone falls and then rises in pitch.

The fourth tone is Ju, the entering tone. The pitch of this tone falls from a higher to a lower level.

The Wade System of Transliteration

CONSONANTS

ch'—as in "church"

'ch—as the "j" in "justice"

k'—as the "k" in "kind"

k—as the "g" in "going"

k'u; k'w—as the "qu" in "quiver"

ku; kw—as the "gu" in "language"

j—as the "s" in "fusion"

p'—as the "p" in "pave"

p—as the "b" in "bath"

t'—as the "t" in "two"

t—as the "d" in "do"

t's—as the "ts" in "boots"

ts—as the "ds" in "leads"

t'z—as the "ts" in "slats"

tz—as the "ds" in "lads"

hs—is pronounced as "sh" in "mesh"

y—as in English when used as a consonant

VOWELS

a—as in "father", except when coming between "w" and "n", and "w" and and "ng", as "wan" and "wang". In this case it is pronounced like the "a" in "want".

ai—as "eye-e"

ao—as "ow" in how"

e—as in "yet"

ei—as the "ey" in "grey"

e—almost like the vowel sound in "turn". Thus "erh" approximates the sound in "err" without the rolled "r". "en" and "eng" have the the same vowel sound as the English "fun" and "hung".

15

i—as the vowel sound in "see". But the sound of "ing" is exactly as in "sing".

ia—as in "piano" when pronounced with the broad "a"

ieh—as the "ie" in siesta" (the "h" does not affect the sound)

ien—as the "ien" in "sienna"

iu—the combination of "i" and of "u" as given below

ih—this sound is quite different from "i"; "ch'ih" like "chi" in "chit" and "shih" as "shir" in "shirk". The final "h" is not sounded; it is merely used to show that the vowel is not the ordinary "i".

o—nearly but not quite so broad as the "aw" in "law"

ou—as in "hoe"

u—as the vowel sound in "too". In "un" and "ung" it is shortened. Thus "sun" is not exactly like "soon" but as though pronounced "soo-n".

ua; uai; uei; ui; uo—these are combinations of "u" with "a", "ai", "ei", "i" and "o" as given above. "ua" comes between "wa" and "oo-a". "uai" comes between "wai" and "oo-ai", etc.

ü—as the "eu" in "Europe"

ŭ—which is only found after "ss" and "tz" is pronounced like the "u" in surrender.

A CONCISE
ENGLISH-CHINESE DICTIONARY

	Chinese	Approximation	Wade
	一	ee[1]	i[1]
ability	能力	nung[2] lee[4]	nêng[2] li[4]
able	能, 能幹	nung[2]; nung[2] gahn[4]	nêng[2]; nêng[2] kan[4]
about (nearly)	大約	dah[4] yew-eh[1]	ta[4] yüeh[1]
abroad	在外	dsy[4] wy[4]	tsai[4] wai[4]
absent	不在	boo[1] dsy[4]	pu[1] tsai[4]
absolute	無限完全	woo[2] shen[4]; wan[2] chew-en[2]	wu[2] hsien[4] wan[2] ch'üan[2]
absolutely	絕對的	jew-eh[2] doo-ee[4] dee[4]	chüeh[2] tui ti[4]
abstract (n)	抽象的	cho[1] she-ang[4] dee[4]	ch'ou[1] hsiang[4] ti[4]
abstract (adj)	提要	tee[2] yaow[4]	t'i[2] yao[4]
abstract (v)	抽出	cho[1] choo[1]	ch'ou[1] ch'u[1]
abundant	豐富	fung[1] foo[4]	fêng[1] fu[4]
abuse (n)	惡習	aw[4] she[2]	o[4] hsi[2]
abuse (v)	妄用	wong[4] yoong[4]	wang[4] yung[4]
accept	接受	jair[1] sho[4]	chieh[1] shou[4]
acceptance	接受	jair[1] sho[4]	chieh[1] shou[4]
accompany	陪	pay[2]	p'ei[2]
accomplish	作成	dsaw[4] chung[2]	tso[4] ch'êng[2]
according to	依照	ed jaow[1]	i[1] chao[1]
account (n)	賬目	jong[4] moo[4]	chang[4] mu[4]
account (v)	說明	shu-aw[1] ming[2]	shuo[1] ming[2]

19

	Chinese	Approximation	Wade
accountant	會計員	whay⁴jee⁴yew-en²	hui⁴chi⁴yüan²
accumulate	積累	jee¹lay³	chi¹lei³
accuse	控告	koong⁴gaow⁴	k'ung⁴kao⁴
accustom	慣	gwan⁴	kuan⁴
ache (n)	痛	toong⁴	t'ung⁴
ache (v)	發痛	fah¹toong⁴	fa¹t'ung⁴
accoustics	聲學	shung¹shoo-er²	shêng¹hsüeh²
across	橫過	hung²gwor⁴	hêng²kuo⁴
acquire	得到	deh²daow⁴	tê²tao⁴
acquisition	得到的	deh²daow⁴dee⁴	tê²tao⁴ti⁴
action	行為	shing²way²	hsing²wei²
actor	戲子	she⁴tze³	hsi⁴tzŭ³
actress	女戲子	nee-u³she⁴tze³	nü³hsi⁴tzŭ³
add	加	jar¹	chia¹
addicted	嗜	shir⁴	shih⁴
addition	加法	jar¹fah³	chia¹fa³
address (n)	地址	dee⁴jih²	ti⁴chih²
address (v)	演說	yen³shu-aw¹	yen³shuo¹
adjust	整理	jung³lee³	chêng³li³
administer	管理	gwan³lee³	kuan³li³
administration	管理	gwan³lee³	kuan³li³

	Chinese	Approximation	Wade
admirable	可羨的	cur³ she-en⁴ dee⁴	k'o³ hsien⁴ ti⁴
admiral	海軍上將	hy³ jew-en¹ shong⁴ je-ong¹	hai³ chün¹ shang⁴ chiang¹
admire	佩服	pay⁴ foo²	p'ei⁴ fu²
admission	入場費	roo⁴ chong² fay⁴	ju⁴ ch'ang² fei⁴
admit	承認准入	chung² run⁴; joo-n³ roo⁴	ch'êng² jên⁴; chun³ ju⁴
admonish	規勸	gway¹ chew-en⁴	kuei¹ ch'üan⁴
advance (n)	進行	jin⁴ shing²	chin⁴ hsing²
advance (v)	前進	chen² jin⁴	ch'ien² chin⁴
advertise	登廣告	dung¹ gwong³ gaow⁴	têng¹ kuang³ kao⁴
advertisement	廣告	gwong³ gaow⁴	kuang³ kao⁴
advice	忠告	joong¹ gaow⁴	chung¹ kao⁴
advise	勸	chwon⁴	ch'uan⁴
affair	事情	shir⁴ ching²	shih⁴ ch'ing²
affidavit	誓詞	shir⁴ tze²	shih⁴ t'zǔ²
afford	出得起	choo¹ deh² chee³	ch'u¹ tê² ch'i³
afraid	怕	pah⁴	p'a⁴
Africa	非洲	fay¹ jo¹	fei¹ chou¹
after	以後	ee³ hoh⁴	i³ hou⁴
afternoon	下午	shah⁴ woo³	hsia⁴ wu³
afterwards	後來	hoh⁴ ly²	hou⁴ lai²
again	再又	dsy⁴ yoo⁴	tsai⁴ yu⁴

	Chinese	Approximation	Wade
age	年齡	ne-en² ling²	nien² ling²
agent	代理人	dy⁴ lee³ run²	tai⁴ li³ jen²
agile	活潑	hwor² paw¹	huo² p'o¹
ago	以前	ee³ chen²	i³ ch'ien²
agree	同意	toong² ee⁴	t'ung² i⁴
agreeable	合意	haw² ee⁴	ho² i⁴
agreement	合同	haw² toong²	ho² t'ung²
aide de camp	副官	foo⁴ gwan¹	fu⁴ kuan¹
air	空氣	koong¹ chee⁴	k'ung¹ ch'i⁴
aircraft	飛機	fay¹ jee¹	fei¹ chi¹
aircraft carrier	飛機母艦	fay¹ jee¹ moo³ chen⁴	fei¹ chi¹ mu³ chien⁴
airplane	飛機	fay¹ jee¹	fei¹ chi¹
airship	飛船	fay¹ chwon²	fei¹ ch'uan²
airy	有空氣	yoo³ koong¹ chee⁴	yu³ k'ung¹ ch'i¹
alarm (n)	警報	jing¹ baow⁴	ching¹ pao⁴
alarm (v)	驚嚇	jing¹ haw⁴	ching¹ ho⁴
alcohol	酒精	je-oo³ jing¹	chiu³ ching¹
alight	落下	law⁴ shah⁴	lo⁴ hsia⁴
alike	一樣	ee¹ yong⁴	i¹ yang⁴
alive	活着	hwar² jaw²	huo² cho²
all	一切,全部	ee¹ chair⁴, chew-en²boo⁴	i¹ ch'ieh⁴, ch'uan² pu⁴

	Chinese	Approximation	Wade
allow	准許	jew-en³ sheu³	chün³ hsü³
allowance	津貼	jing¹ tee-air¹	ching¹ t'ieh¹
almanac	曆書	lee⁴ shoo¹	li⁴ shu¹
almost	差不多	chah¹ boo² daw¹	ch'a¹ pu² to¹
alone	單獨	don¹ doo²	tan¹ tu²
already	已經	ee³ jing¹	i³ ching¹
also	也又	yair³; yoo⁴	yeh³; yu⁴
alter	更改	gung¹ guy³	kêng¹ kai³
alteration	改變	guy¹ be-en⁴	kai¹ pien⁴
alternate	輪流	loo-en² le-oo²	lun² liu²
alternative	二中擇一	er⁴ joong¹ tser² ee²	êrh⁴ chung¹ ts'ê² i²
although	雖然	shway¹ rahn²	sui¹ jan²
always	常常	chong² chong²	ch'ang² ch'ang²
ambition	志向	jir⁴ she-ong⁴	chih⁴ hsiang⁴
ambulance	救護車	je-oo⁴ hoo⁴ chair¹	chiu⁴ hu⁴ ch'ê¹
America	美國	may³ gwor²	mei³ kuo²
American (adj)	美國的	may³ gwor² dee⁴	mei³ kuo² ti⁴
American (n)	美國人	may³ gwor² run²	mei³ kuo² jên²
among	在內	dsy⁴ nay⁴	tsai⁴ nei⁴
ample	充足	choong¹ dsoo²	ch'ung¹ tsu²
ammunition	軍火	jew-en¹ hwor²	chün¹ huo²

	Chinese	Approximation	Wade
ammunition wagon	軍火車	jew-en¹ hwor² chair¹	chün¹ huo² ch'ê¹
amuse	消遣	she-aow¹ chen³	hsiao¹ ch'ien³
amusement	娛樂趣	yeu² law⁴	yü² lo⁴
amusing	有趣	yoo³ choo⁴	yu³ ch'u⁴
analysis	分析	fun¹ she⁴	fên¹ hsi⁴
analyze	分析	fun¹ she⁴	fên¹ hsi⁴
ancestor	祖宗	dsoo³ dsoong¹	tsu³ tsung¹
anchor (n)	錨	maow²	mao²
anchor (v)	拋錨	paow¹ maow²	p'ao¹ mao²
ancient	古, 老	goo³; laow³	ku³; lao³
and	和, 同	haw³; toong²	ho³; t'ung²
anger (n)	怒	noo⁴	nu⁴
angle	角	jew-eh²	chüeh²
animal	動物	doong⁴ woo⁴	tung⁴ wu⁴
announce	傳報	chwan² baow⁴	ch'uan² pao⁴
announcement	佈告	boo⁴ gaow⁴	pu⁴ kao⁴
annoy	煩擾	fahn² raow³	fan² jao³
annoyance	煩惱	fahn² naow³	fan² nao³
another	另一	ling⁴ ee¹	ling⁴ i¹
answer (n)	答復	dah² foo²	ta² fu²
answer (v)	答復	dah² foo²	ta² fu²

	Chinese	Approximation	Wade
ant	螞 蟻	mah^3 ee^1	ma^3 i^1
anticipate	預 料	yeu^4 le-aow^4	yü^4 liao^4
anticipation	預 料	yeu^4 le-aow^4	yü^4 liao^4
antique (n)	古 物	goo^3 woo^4	ku^3 wu^4
antique (adj)	古 的	goo^3 dee^1	ku^3 ti^1
anxiety	憂 慮	yoo^1 leu^4	yu^1 lü^4
anxious	不 安	boo^1 ahn^1	pu^1 an^1
any	任 何	run^4 haw^2	jên^4 ho^2
apologize	道 歉	daow^4 jen^4	tao^4 chien^4
apology	道 歉	daow^4 jen^4	tao^4 chien^4
apparent	顯 明	she-en^3 ming^2	hsien^3 ming^2
apparently	顯 明 的	she-en^3 ming^2 dee^1	hsien^3 ming^2 ti^1
appetite	味 口	way^4 koh^3	wei^4 k'ou^3
apple	蘋 果	pin^2 gwor^3	p'in^2 kuo^3
application	請 求 書	ching^3 che-oo^2 shoo^1	ch'ing^3 ch'iu^2 shu^1
apply	請 求	ching^3 che-oo^2	ch'ing^3 ch'iu^2
appoint	派	py^4	p'ai^4
appointment	任 命	run^4 ming^4	jên^4 ming^4
appropriate	合 宜	haw^2 ee^4	ho^2 i^4
approximate	近 似	jin^4 sze^4	chin^4 ssŭ^4
apricot	杏	shing^4	hsing^4

	Chinese	Approximation	Wade
April	四月	sze^4 yew-eh^4	ssŭ^4 yüeh^4
architect	建築家	je-en^4 dsoo^2 jar^1	chien^4 tsu^2 chia^1
arise	起來	chee^3 ly^2	ch'i^3 lai^2
arrival	來到	ly^2 daow^4	lai^2 tao^4
arm (n)	臂	bay^4	pei^4
arithmetic	算法	swon^4 fah^3	suan^4 fa^3
armistice	休戰	sheoo^1 jahn^4	hsiu^1 chan^4
arms (small)	武器	woo^3 chee^4	wu^3 ch'i^4
army	軍隊	jew-en^1 dway^4	chün^1 tui^4
army corps	軍隊	jew-en^1 dway^4	chün^1 tui^4
around	週圍	jo^1 way^2	chou^1 wei^2
arouse	激動	jee^2 doong^4	chi^2 tung^4
arrange	佈置	boo^4 jir^4	pu^4 chih^4
arrangement	佈置	boo^4 jir^4	pu^4 chih^4
arrears	欠欵	chen^4 kwan^3	ch'ien^4 k'uan^3
arrest	捉拿	jaw^1 nah^2	cho^1 na^2
arrive	到	daow^4	tao^4
arrow	箭	je-en^4	chien^4
arsenal	兵工廠	bing^1 goong^1 chong^3	ping^1 kung^1 ch'ang^3
art	美術	may^3 shoo^4	mei^3 shu^4
artillery	炮隊	paow^4 dway^4	p'ao^4 tui^4

	Chinese	Approximation	Wade
artist	美術家	may³ shoo⁴ jar¹	mei³ shu⁴ chia¹
as	如同	roo² toong²	ju² tung²
ascend	登	dung¹	têng¹
ascent	登高	dung¹ gaow¹	têng¹ kao¹
ashes	灰	whay¹	hui¹
Asia	亞洲	yah⁴ joh¹	ya⁴ chou¹
Asiatic	亞洲的	yah⁴ joh¹ dee¹	ya⁴ chou¹ ti¹
ask	問	wun⁴	wên⁴
aspect	方向	fong¹ she-ong⁴	fang¹ hsiang⁴
assemble	會集	whay⁴ jee²	hui⁴ chi²
assembly	集會	jee² whay⁴	chi² hui⁴
asset	財產	tsy² jahn³	ts'ai² ch'an³
assist	協助	she-eh² joo⁴	hsieh² chu⁴
assistance	援助	yew-en² joo⁴	yüan² chu⁴
assure	擔保	dahn⁴ baow³	tan⁴ pao³
assurance	擔保	dahn⁴ baow³	tan⁴ pao³
astronomer	天文家	te-en¹ wun² jar¹	t'ien¹ wên² chia¹
astronomy	天文學	te-en¹ wun² shoo-er²	t'ien¹ wên² hsüeh²
astute	聰明	tsoong¹ ming²	tsung¹ ming²
astuteness	聰明	tsoong¹ ming²	tsung¹ ming²
at	在於	dsy⁴; yeu²	tsai⁴; yü²

	Chinese	Approximation	Wade
at last	最後	dsoo-ee⁴ hoh⁴	tsui⁴ hou⁴
Atlantic Ocean	大西洋	dah⁴ she¹ yong²	ta⁴ hsi¹ yang²
atmosphere	空氣	koong¹ chee⁴	k'ung¹ ch'i⁴
attack (n)	攻擊	goong¹ jee²	kung¹ chi²
attack (v)	攻擊	goong¹ jee²	kung¹ chi²
attend	當心	dong¹ shin¹	tang¹ hsin¹
attention	注意	joo⁴ ee⁴	chu⁴ i⁴
August	八月	bah² yew-eh⁴	pa² yüeh⁴
aunt	姑娘	goo¹; ee²	ku¹; i²
auspicious	吉利	jee² lee⁴	chi² li⁴
austere	嚴格	yen² gur²	yen² ko²
austerity	嚴厲	yen² lee⁴	yen² li⁴
author	作家	dsaw² jar¹	tso² chia¹
authority	主權	joo³ chwon²	chu³ ch'uan²
authorize	准	joo-n³	chun³
autocracy	專制	joo-an¹ jir⁴	chuan¹ chih⁴
automobile	汽車	chee⁴ chair¹	ch'i⁴ ch'ê¹
autumn	秋天	che-oo¹ te-en¹	ch'iu¹ t'ien¹
avenge	報仇	baow⁴ choh²	pao⁴ ch'ou²
awaken	喚醒	whon⁴ shing³	huan⁴ hsing³
awkward	笨拙的	bun⁴ jaw¹ dee¹	pên⁴ cho¹ ti¹

28

	Chinese	Approximation	Wade
axe	斧子	foo³ tze³	fu³ tzŭ³
axis	軸心	joh² shin¹	chou² hsin¹

B

	Chinese	Approximation	Wade
baby	嬰兒	ying¹ er²	ying¹ êrh²
back	背後	bay⁴ hoh⁴	pei⁴ hou⁴
bacon	火腿	hwor³ too-ee³	huo³ t'ui³
bad	惡,壞	aw³; why⁴	o³; huai⁴
bag	袋	dy⁴	tai⁴
baggage	行李	shing² lee³	hsing² li³
bake	烤,烘	kaow³; hoong¹	k'ao³; hung¹
balance	天秤	tee-en¹ chung⁴	t'ien¹ ch'êng⁴
ball	球	che-oo²	ch'iu²
bamboo	竹	joo²	chu²
bandage	繃帶	bung² dy⁴	pêng² tai⁴
bank	銀行	yin² hong²	yin² hang²
banquet	酒席	jee-oo³ she²	chiu³ hsi²
baptize	受洗禮	sho⁴ she³ lee³	shou⁴ hsi³ li³
baptism	受洗禮	she³ lee³	hsi³ li³
barber	理髮匠	lee³ fah² je-ong⁴	li³ fa² chiang⁴
bare	赤裸	chir⁴ law³	ch'ih⁴ lo³
bark (n)	樹皮,狗叫	shoo⁴ pee²; goh² je-aow⁴	shu⁴ p'i²; kou² chiao⁴

	Chinese	Approximation	Wade
bark (v)	狗叫	goh² je-aow⁴	kou² chiao⁴
barley	大麥	dah⁴ my⁴	ta⁴ mai⁴
barometer	風雨表	fung¹ yeu³ be-aow³	fêng¹ yü³ piao³
barracks	兵營	bing² ying²	ping² ying²
barter	換貨	whon⁴ hwor⁴	huan⁴ huo⁴
bashful	怕羞	pah⁴ she-oo¹	p'a⁴ hsiu¹
basis	根本	gun¹ bun³	kên¹ pên³
basket	籃筐	lahn²; kwong¹	lan²; k'uang¹
bath	洗澡	she³ dsaow³	hsi³ tsao³
bathe	洗澡	she³ dsaow³	hsi³ tsao³
battleship	戰船	jahn⁴ chwon²	chan⁴ ch'uan²
battery (electric)	電池	de-en⁴ chir²	tien⁴ ch'ih²
battle	交戰	je-aow¹ jahn⁴	chiao¹ chan⁴
bay	海灣	hy³ wahn¹	hai³ wan¹
bayonet	刺刀	tze⁴ daow¹	t'zŭ⁴ tao¹
be	是 為 在	shir²; way²; dsy⁴	shih²; wei²; tsai⁴
beach	海灘	hy³ tahn¹	hai³ t'an¹
bean	豆	doh⁴	tou⁴
bear (v)	忍受	run³ sho⁴	jên³ shou⁴
beat	打	dah³	ta³
beautiful	美	may³	mei³

	Chinese	Approximation	Wade
because	因為	yin¹ way⁴	yin¹ wei⁴
become	成為	chung² way⁴	ch'êng² wei⁴
bed	牀	chwong³	ch'uang²
bedclothes	舖蓋	poo¹ guy⁴	p'u¹ kai⁴
bedroom	臥室	woh⁴ shir²	wo⁴ shih²
bee	蜂	fung¹	fêng¹
beetle	甲蟲	jar² choong²	chia² ch'ung²
beef	牛肉	nee-u² roh⁴	niu² jou⁴
beer	啤酒	pee² je-oo³	p'i² chiu³
before	先，前	she-en¹; che-en²	hsien¹; ch'ien²
beg	請求	ching³ che-oo²	ch'ing³ ch'iu²
begin	開始	ky¹ shir³	k'ai¹ shih³
behave	動作	doong⁴ dsaw⁴	tung⁴ tso⁴
behavior	行為	shing² way²	hsing² wei²
behind	在後	dsy⁴ hoh⁴	tsai⁴ hou⁴
belief	信仰	shin⁴ yong³	hsin⁴ yang³
believe	相信	she-ong¹ shin⁴	hsiang¹ hsin⁴
believer	信仰的	shin⁴ yong³ dee¹	hsin⁴ yang³ ti¹
bell	鈴，鐘	ling²; joong¹	ling²; chung¹
belly	肚子	doo⁴ tze³	tu⁴ tzŭ³
below	下面	shah⁴ me-en⁴	hsia⁴ mien⁴

	Chinese		Approximation	Wade
belt	腰	帶	yaow¹ dy⁴	yao¹ tai⁴
bench	長	凳	chong² dung⁴	ch'ang² têng⁴
bend (n)	彎		wan¹	wan¹
bend (v)	使	彎	shir³ wan¹	shih³ wan¹
beneath	在	下	dsy⁴ shah⁴	tsai⁴ hsia⁴
benefit (n)	利	益	lee⁴ ee²	li⁴ i²
benefit (v)	有	益	yoo³ ee²	yu³ i²
bent	彎	曲	wan³ cheu¹	wan³ ch'ü¹
beri-beri	腳	氣病	jaow³ chee⁴ bing⁴	chiao³ ch'i⁴ ping⁴
Berlin	柏	林	baw⁴ lin²	po⁴ lin²
besides	外	加,又	wy⁴ jar'; yoo⁴	wai⁴ chia'; yu⁴
best	最	好的	dsoo-ee⁴ haow³ dee'	tsui⁴ hao³ ti'
better	更	好的	gung⁴ haow³ dee'	kêng⁴ hao³ ti'
between	在	中間	dsy⁴ joong¹ che-en¹	tsai⁴ chung¹ ch'ien'
beyond	以	外	ee³ wy⁴	i³ wai⁴
Bible	聖	經	shung⁴ jing'	shêng⁴ ching'
bicycle	腳	踏車	je-aow³ tah⁴ chair'	chiao³ t'a⁴ ch'ê'
big	大		dah⁴	ta⁴
bill	賬		jong⁴	chang⁴
biology	生	物學	shung¹ woo⁴ shoo-er²	shêng¹ wu⁴ hsüeh²
bird	鳥		nee-aow³	niao³

	Chinese	Approximation	Wade
birth	生	shung¹	shêng¹
birthday	生日	shung¹ rih⁴	shêng¹ jih⁴
biscuit	餅乾	bing³ gahn¹	ping³ kan¹
bite (n)	咬傷	yaow³ shong¹	yao³ shang¹
bite (v)	咬	yaow³	yao³
bitter	苦	koo³	k'u³
bitterness	苦味	koo³ way⁴	k'u³ wei⁴
black	黑	hay¹	hei¹
blame (n)	過失	gwor⁴ shir²	kuo⁴ shih²
blame (v)	受責	sho⁴ dser²	shou⁴ tsê²
blank	空白	koong¹ by²	k'ung¹ pai²
blanket	毯子	tahn³ tze³	t'an³ tzŭ³
bleed	出血	choo¹ shoo-er³	ch'u¹ hsüeh³
blend	調和	te-aow² haw²	t'iao² ho²
blind	瞎眼	shah¹ yen³	hsia¹ yen³
blood	血	shoo-er³	hsüeh³
bloom	開花	ky¹ whah¹	k'ai¹ hua¹
blow	吹	choo-ee¹	ch'ui¹
blue	藍	lahn²	lan²
board	木板	moo⁴ bahn³	mu⁴ pan³
boast (v)	誇張	kwah¹ jong¹	k'ua¹ chang¹

33

	Chinese	Approximation	Wade
boat	船	chwon²	ch'uan²
boatman	船夫	chwon² foo¹	ch'uan² fu¹
body	身體	shun¹ tee³	shên¹ ti³
boil (v)	煮	joo¹	chu¹
bomb (n)	炸彈	jar⁴ dahn⁴	cha⁴ tan⁴
bomb (v)	丟炸彈	dee-oo¹ jar⁴ dahn⁴	tiu¹ cha⁴ tan⁴
bombard	砲轟	paow⁴ hoong¹	p'ao⁴ hung¹
bone	骨頭	goo³ doh²	ku³ tou²
book	書	shoo¹	shu¹
bookseller	賣書的	my³ shoo¹ dee¹	mai³ shu¹ ti¹
border	邊界	be-en¹ jair⁴	pien¹ chieh⁴
borrow	借	jair⁴	chieh⁴
both	兩個	le-ong⁴ gur⁴	liang⁴ ko⁴
bottle	瓶	ping²	p'ing²
bottom	底	dee³	ti³
boulevard	大街	dah⁴ jair¹	ta⁴ chieh¹
boundary	境界	jing⁴ jair⁴	ching⁴ chieh⁴
bow (n)	鞠躬	jeu² goong¹	chü² kung¹
bow (v)	鞠躬	jeu² goong¹	chü² kung¹
bowl	碗	wahn³	wan³
box	箱匣	she-ong¹; shah³	hsiang¹; hsia³

34

	Chinese		Approximation	Wade
boy	男孩		nahn² hy²	nan² hai²
brag	吹牛		choo-ee¹ nee-u²	ch'ui¹ niu²
brain	腦		naow³	nao³
branch	樹枝 支派		shoo³ jir¹; jir¹ py⁴	shu³ chih¹; chih¹ p'ai⁴
brandy	白蘭地酒		baw² lahn² dee¹ jee-oo³	po² lan² ti¹ chiu³
brass	銅		toong²	t'ung²
brave	勇敢		yoong³ gahn³	yung³ kan³
bread	麵包		me-en⁴ baow¹	mien⁴ pao¹
break (n)	破碎		paw⁴ shway⁴	p'o⁴ shui⁴
break (v)	打破		dah² paw⁴	ta² p'o⁴
breakfast	早飯		dsaow³ fahn⁴	tsao³ fan⁴
break new soil	墾		gun³	kên³
breath	氣息		chee⁴ she⁴	ch'i⁴ hsi⁴
breathe	呼吸		hoo⁴ she⁴	hu⁴ hsi⁴
breed	產		chahn³	ch'an³
bride	新婦		shin¹ foo⁴	hsin¹ fu⁴
bridge	橋		che-aow²	ch'iao²
brief	簡短		je-en³ dwon³	chien³ tuan³
brigade	旅隊		leu³; doo-ee³	lü³; tui³
bright	光明		gwong¹ ming²	kuang¹ ming²
bring	拿來		nah² ly²	na² lai²

35

	Chinese	Approximation	Wade
broad	寬大	kwan¹ dah⁴	k'uan¹ ta⁴
broken	破裂	paw⁴le-air⁴	p'o⁴ lieh⁴
broom	掃把	saow⁴ bah³	sao⁴ pa³
brother (elder)	哥哥	gur⁴ gur⁴	ko⁴ ko⁴
brother (younger)	弟弟	dee⁴ dee⁴	ti⁴ ti⁴
brother-in-law	姐夫 妹夫	jair³ foo'; may⁴ foo'	chieh³ fu'; mei⁴ fu'
brown	深黃	shun¹ whong²	shên¹ huang²
bruise	傷	shong¹	shang¹
brush (n)	毛刷	maow² shwah¹	mao² shua¹
brush (v)	刷	shwah¹	shua¹
buddha	佛	faw²	fo²
budget	預算	yeu⁴ swon⁴	yü⁴ suan⁴
bugle	喇叭	lah³ bah¹	la³ pa¹
build	建築	je-ən⁴ joo²	chien⁴ chu²
building	房屋	fahng² woo¹	fang² wu¹
bulky	大	dah⁴	ta⁴
bull	公牛	goong¹ nee-u²	kung¹ niu²
bullet	槍彈	che-ong¹ dahn⁴	ch'iang¹ tan⁴
bully	莽漢	mong³ hahn⁴	mang³ han⁴
burn (n)	燒焦	she-aow¹ jaow¹	hsiao¹ chiao¹
burn (v)	燒焦	she-aow¹ jaow¹	hsiao¹ chiao¹

	Chinese	Approximation	Wade
burnt	燒焦的	she-aow¹ jaow¹ dee¹	hsiao¹ chiao¹ ti¹
burst	爆裂	baow⁴ le-air⁴	pao⁴ lieh⁴
bury	掩埋	yen³ my³	yen³ mai³
burial	葬	dsong⁴	tsang⁴
business	事務	shir⁴ woo⁴	shih⁴ wu⁴
busy	忙	mong²	mang²
but	可是但	cur³ shir⁴; dahn⁴	k'o³ shih⁴; tan⁴
butcher	屠夫	too² foo¹	t'u² fu¹
butter	牛油	nee-u² yoo²	niu² yu²
butterfly	蝴蝶	hoo² de-air⁴	hu² tieh⁴
button	細扣	nee-u³ koh⁴	niu³ k'ou⁴
buy	買	my³	mai³
buyer	買主	my³ joo³	mai³ chu³
by and by	不久	boo¹ je-oo³	pu¹ chiu³
by degrees	漸漸	je-en⁴ je-en⁴	chien⁴ chien⁴
by hand	用手	yoong⁴ sho³	yung⁴ chou³
c			
cabbage	白菜	by² dsy⁴	pai² tsai⁴
cabin	小屋,船艙	sheaow³ woo³; chwon² tsong¹	hsiao³ wu³; ch'uan² ts'ang¹
cake	餅,餻	bing³; gaow¹	ping³; kao¹
calamity	災難	dsy¹ nahn²	tsai¹ nan²

		Chinese	Approximation	Wade
calculate	計算	jee⁴ swon⁴	chi⁴ suan⁴
calculation	計算	jee⁴ swon⁴	chi⁴ suan⁴
calendar	日曆	rih⁴ lee⁴	jih⁴ li⁴
call (n)	叫,喊,訪問	je-aow⁴; hoo⁴; fong³ wun⁴	chiao⁴; hu⁴; fang³ wên⁴
call (v)	叫,喊,訪問	je-aow⁴; hoo⁴; fong³ wun⁴	chiao⁴; hu⁴; fang³ wên⁴
calligraphy	書法	shoo' fah³	shu' fa³
calm	安靜	ahn' jing⁴	an' ching⁴
camera	照相機	jaow' she-ong⁴ jee'	chao' hsiang⁴ chi'
camp (n)	營地	ying² dee⁴	ying² ti⁴
camp (v)	紮營	jah' ying²	cha' ying²
camping ground	營地	ying² dee⁴	ying² ti⁴
can	能可以	nung²; cur³ ee³	nêng²; k'o³ i³
canal	運河	yew-n⁴ haw²	yün⁴ ho²
cancel	取消	choo³ she-aow'	ch'u³ hsiao'
cancellation	取消	choo³ she-aow'	ch'u³ hsiao'
candle	蠟燭	lah⁴ joo²	la⁴ chu²
candy	糖食	tong² shir²	t'ang² shih²
cannon	炮	paow⁴	p'ao⁴
cap	帽子	maow⁴ tze³	mao⁴ tzŭ³
capacity	才能	tsy² nung²	t'sai² nêng²
capital	京城	jing' chung²	ching' ch'êng²

	Chinese	Approximation	Wade
captain (army)	陸軍上尉	loo⁴ jew-en¹ shong⁴ way⁴	lu⁴ chün¹ shang⁴ wei¹⁴
captain (navy)	海軍上尉	hy³ jew-en¹ shong⁴ way⁴	hai³ chün¹ shang⁴ wei¹⁴
capture	捕獲	boo² hwor²	pu² huo²
car	車	chair¹	ch'ê¹
carbolic acid	石炭酸	shir² tahn⁴ swon¹	shih² t'an⁴ suan¹
carcass	屍首	shir¹ sho³	shih¹ shou³
care (n)	管注意	gwan³; joo⁴ ee⁴	kuan³; chu⁴ i⁴
care (v)	管注意	gwan³; joo⁴ ee⁴	kuan³; chu⁴ i⁴
careful	留意小心	lee-oo² ee⁴; she-aow³ shin¹	liu² i⁴; hsiao³ hsin¹
careless	不小心	boo¹ she-aow³ shin¹	pu¹ hsiao³ hsin¹
cargo	貨物	hwor⁴ woo⁴	huo⁴ wu⁴
carpenter	木匠	moo⁴ jong⁴	mu⁴ chiang⁴
carpentry	木工	moo⁴ goong¹	mu⁴ kung¹
carpet	地毯	dee⁴ tahn³	ti⁴ t'an³
carriage	馬車	mah³ chair¹	ma³ ch'ê¹
carrot	紅蘿蔔	hoong² law² baw⁴	hung² lo² po⁴
carry	帶擔抱	dy⁴; dahn¹; baow⁴	tai⁴; tan¹; pao⁴
cart	大車	dah⁴ chair¹	ta⁴ ch'ê¹
cartridge	子彈	tze³ dahn⁴	tzŭ³ tan⁴
cash	現錢	she-en⁴ chen²	hsien⁴ ch'ien²
cat	貓	maow²	mao²

	Chinese	Approximation	Wade
catalogue (n)	目錄	moo⁴ loo⁴	mu⁴ lu⁴
catalogue (v)	編目錄	be-en¹ moo⁴ loo⁴	pien¹ mu⁴ lu⁴
catch	挺拿	jaw² nah²	cho² na²
Catholic	天主教	te-en¹ joo³ je-aow¹	t'ien¹ chu³ chiao¹
cattle	牛家畜	nee-u³; jar¹ choo²	niu³; chia¹ ch'u²
cauliflower	花菜	whah¹ tsy⁴	hua¹ ts'ai⁴
cause (n)	原因	yew-en² yin¹	yüan² yin¹
cause (v)	使令	shir³; ling⁴	shih³; ling⁴
cautious	當心	dong¹ shin¹	tang¹ hsin¹
cavalry	馬隊	mah³ doo-ee⁴	ma³ tui⁴
cave	洞	doong⁴	tung⁴
cease	停止	ting²; jir³	t'ing²; chih³
ceaseless	不停	boo¹ ting²	p'u¹ t'ing²
cede	讓給	rong⁴ gay³	jang⁴ kei³
ceiling	天花板	te-en¹ whah¹ bahn³	t'ien¹ hua¹ pan³
cellar	地窖	dee⁴ gaow⁴	ti⁴ kao⁴
cement	水泥	shway³ nee²	shui³ ni²
cemetery	墓地墳地	moo⁴ dee¹; fun² dee¹	mu⁴ ti¹; fên² ti¹
cent	分	fun¹	fên¹
center	中心	joong¹ shin¹	chung¹ hsin¹
century	百年世紀	by³ ne-en³; shir⁴ jir⁴	pai³ nien³; shih⁴ chih⁴

	Chinese	Approximation	Wade
certain	一定	ee² ding⁴	i ting
certainly	一定	ee² ding⁴	i ting
certainty	的確	dee⁴ chew-eh⁴	ti ch'üeh
certificate	證書	jung⁴ shoo¹	chêng shu
chain	鎖鏈	saw² le-en⁴	so lien
chair	椅子	ee³ tze³	i tzŭ
chalk	粉筆	fun³ bee¹	fên pi
chamber	房間	fahng³ je-en¹	fang chien
chamber of commerce	商會	shong¹ whay⁴	shang hui
chance	機會	jee¹ whay⁴	chi hui
change (n)	變更	be-en⁴ gung¹	pien kêng
change (v)	改變	guy³ be-en⁴	kai pien
character	性質	shing⁴ jee²	hsing chi
character (Chinese)	字	tze⁴	tzŭ
charge (price)	定價	ding⁴ jar⁴	ting chia
charge (accuse)	歸罪	gway¹ dsoo-ee⁴	kuei tsui
charge (military)	攻	goong¹	kung
charge (load)	裝量	jwong¹ le-ong⁴	chuang liang
charity	博愛	baw² ai⁴	po ai
charm	魔力	maw² lee⁴	mo li
chart (n)	地圖	dee¹ too²	ti t'u

	Chinese	Approximation	Wade
chase (v)	追趕	choo-ee¹ gahn³	chui¹ kan³
chat (v)	閒談	she-en² tahn²	hsien² t'an²
cheat (v)	欺騙	chee¹ pe-en⁴	ch'i¹ p'ien⁴
check (bank)	支票	jir¹ peaow⁴	chih¹ p'iao⁴
cheek	面頰	me-en⁴ jar²	mien⁴ chia²
cheerful	快活	kwy⁴ hwor²	k'uai⁴ huo²
cheese	乳酪	roo³ law²	ju³ lo²
chemist	化學家	whah⁴ shoo-er² jar¹	hua⁴ hsüeh² chia¹
chemistry	化學	whah⁴ shoo-er²	hua⁴ hsüeh²
cherish	保護	baow³ hoo⁴	pao³ hu⁴
cherry	櫻桃	ying¹ taow²	ying¹ t'ao²
chest	箱櫃子	she-ong¹; gway⁴tze³	hsiang¹; kuei⁴tzŭ³
chess	棋	chee²	ch'i²
chicken	小鷄	she-aow³ jee¹	hsiao³ chi¹
child	小孩	she-aow³ hy²	hsiao³ hai²
children	孩子們	hy² tze³ mun²	hai² tzŭ³ mên²
chill	涼,冷	le-ong²; lung³	liang²; lêng³
chilly	涼冷	le-ong²; lung³	liang²; lêng³
chimney	煙囪	yen¹ chwong¹	yen¹ ch'uang¹
China	中國	joong¹ gwor²	chung¹ kuo²
chinaware	磁器	tze² chee⁴	tz'ŭ² ch'i⁴

	Chinese	Approximation	Wade
Chinese (adj)	中國的	joong¹ gwor² dee¹	chung¹ kuo² ti¹
Chinese (n)	中國人	joong¹ gwor² run²	chung¹ kuo² jên²
chocolate	巧格力糖	che-aow³ gur² lee⁴ tong²	ch'iao³ ko² li⁴ t'ang²
choice	選擇	shew-an³ dser²	hs'üan³ tsê²
Cholera	霍亂	haw⁴ lu-wan⁴	ho⁴ luan⁴
choose	選擇	shew-an³ dser²	hs'üan³ tsê²
chopsticks	筷子	kwy⁴ tze³	k'uai⁴ tzŭ³
Christ	耶蘇	yeh³ soo¹	yeh³ su¹
Christian	耶蘇教徒	yeh³ soo¹ je-aow⁴ too²	yeh³ su¹ chiao⁴ t'u²
Christianity	耶蘇教	yeh³ soo¹ je-aow⁴	yeh³ su¹ chiao⁴
Christmas	聖誕節	shung⁴ dahn⁴ jair²	shêng⁴ tan⁴ chieh²
chum	好友	haow³ yoo³	hao³ yu³
church	禮拜堂	lee³ by⁴ tahng²	li³ pai⁴ t'ang²
cigar	雪茄煙	shoo-er² chair¹ yen¹	hsüeh² ch'ieh¹ yen¹
cigarette	煙捲	yen¹ jwan³	yen¹ chuan³
circle (n)	圓圈	yew-en² chew-en¹	yüan² ch'üan¹
circulate	流通	lee-oo² toong¹	liu² t'ung¹
circumscribe	限制	she-en⁴ tze⁴	hsien⁴ tz'ŭ⁴
circumspect	謹慎	jin³ shun⁴	chin³ shên⁴
circumstance	情形	ching² shing²	ch'ing² hsing²
circus	馬戲	mah³ she⁴	ma³ hsi⁴

43

	Chinese	Approximation	Wade
cistern	水缸	shway³ gong¹	shui³ kang¹
citizen	國民	gwor² min²	kuo² min²
city	城市	chung² shir⁴	ch'êng² shih⁴
civil	文的	wun² dee¹	wên² ti¹
civilize	開化	ky¹ whah⁴	k'ai¹ hua⁴
civilized	開化的	ky¹ whah⁴ dee	k'ai¹ hua⁴ ti
civilization	文明	wun² ming²	wên² ming²
clarify	說明	shoo-aw¹ ming²	shuo¹ ming²
class (n)	種類	joong³ lay⁴	chung³ lei⁴
classic	經書	jing¹ shoo¹	ching¹ shu¹
classification	分類	fun¹ lay⁴	fên¹ lei⁴
classifier (general N.A.) 個		gur⁴	ko⁴
classify	分類	fun¹ lay⁴	fên¹ lei⁴
classmate	同班	toong² bahn	t'ung² pan¹
classroom	課室	cur⁴ shir⁴	k'o⁴ shih⁴
clause	條欵	te-aow² kwon³	t'iao² k'uan³
clay	泥土	nee² too³	ni² t'u³
clean (adj)	清潔	ching¹ jair²	ch'ing¹ chieh²
clean (v)	洗淨	she³ jing⁴	hsi³ ching⁴
cleanliness	清潔	ching¹ jair²	ch'ing¹ chieh²
clear (adj)	明白	ming² by²	ming² pai²

44

English	Chinese	Approximation	Wade
clerk	書記	shoo4 jee4	shu4 chi4
clever	靈巧	ling1 che-aow3	ling1 ch'iao3
cliff	石巖	shir2 yen3	shih2 yen3
climate	氣候	chee4 hoh4	ch'i4 hou4
climb (v)	爬上去	pah3 shong4	p'a3 shang4
clip	剪去	jee-n1 chew4	chien1 ch'ü4
clock	鐘	joong1	chung1
close	關	gwan1	kuan1
cloth	布	boo4	pu4
clothes	衣服	ee1 foo2	i1 fu2
cloud	雲	yew-n2	yün2
club	總會	dsoong3 whay4	tsung3 hui4
coal	煤	may2	mei2
coast	海岸	hy3 ahn4	hai3 an4
coat	外衣	wy4 ee1	wai4 i1
cork	軟木	roo-on3 moo4	juan3 mu4
coffee	咖啡	kah1 fay1	k'a1 fei1
coffin	棺材	gwan1 tsy2	kuan1 ts'ai2
cold	冷	lung3	lêng3
collapse (v)	倒下	daow3 shah4	tao3 hsia4
collar	領子	ling3 tze3	ling3 tzŭ3

	Chinese	Approximation	Wade
collect	收集	sho¹ jee²	shou¹ chi²
college	大學	dah⁴ shoo-er²	ta⁴ hsüeh²
collide	相碰	she-ong¹ pung⁴	hsiang¹ p'êng⁴
collision	衝突	choong¹ too²	ch'ung¹ t'u²
colonel	陸軍上校	loo² jew-en¹ shong⁴ je-aow⁴	lu² chün¹ shang⁴ chiao⁴
color	顏色	yen² ser⁴	yen² sê⁴
colorless	無色的	woo² ser⁴ dee¹	wu² sê⁴ ti¹
column	柱子	joo⁴ tze²	chu⁴ tzŭ³
comb	梳子	shoo¹ tze³	shu¹ tzŭ³
combat (v)	爭鬥	jung¹ doh⁴	chêng¹ tou⁴
combatant	爭鬥者	jung¹ doh⁴ jaw³	chêng¹ tou⁴ chê³
come	來	ly²	lai²
comet	彗星	saow⁴ shing¹	sao⁴ hsing¹
comfort	安樂	ahn¹ law⁴	an¹ lo⁴
comfortable	舒服	shoo¹ foo²	shu¹ fu²
command (n)	命令	ming⁴ ling⁴	ming⁴ ling⁴
command (v)	命令	ming⁴ ling⁴	ming⁴ ling⁴
commander	長官	jong³ gwan¹	chang³ kuan¹
commander-in-chief	總司令	dsoong³ sze¹ ling⁴	tsung³ ssŭ¹ ling⁴
commerce	商務	shong¹ woo⁴	shang¹ wu⁴
committee	委員會	way³ yoo-an² whay⁴	wei³ yuan² hui⁴

	Chinese	Approximation	Wade
common	普通	poo³ toong¹	p'u³ t'ung¹
communism	共產主義	goong⁴ chahn³ joo³ ee⁴	kung⁴ ch'an³ chu³ i⁴
communist	共產主義者	goong⁴ chahn³ joo³ ee⁴ jaw³	kung⁴ ch'an³ chu³ i⁴ chê³
community	社會	sher⁴ whay⁴	shê⁴ hui⁴
companion	同伴	toong² bahn¹	t'ung² pan¹
company	公司	goong¹ sze¹	kung¹ ssŭ¹
comparative	比較	bee³ jaow³	pi³ chao³
comparatively	比較的	bee³ jaow³ dee¹	pi³ chao³ ti¹
compare	比較	bee³ jaow³	pi³ chao³
comparison	比較	bee³ jaow³	pi³ chao³
compass	指南針	jair³ nahn² jen¹	chieh³ nan² chen¹
compel	強迫	che-ong³ baw⁴	ch'iang³ po⁴
compensate	賠償	pay² shong¹	p'ei² shang²
compensation	賠償	pay² shong²	p'ei² shang²
compete	比賽	bee³ sy⁴	pi³ sai⁴
competition	比賽	bee³ sy⁴	pi³ sai⁴
complete	完全	wahn² chew-en²	wan² ch'üan²
comply	依從	ee¹ tsoong²	i¹ ts'ung²
compose	作文	dsaw⁴ wun²	tso⁴ wên²
composition	文章	wun² jong¹	wên² chang¹
compound	合成的	haw² chung² dee¹	ho² ch'êng² ti¹

	Chinese	Approximation	Wade
compromise (n)	和解	haw² jair³	ho² chieh³
compromise (v)	和解	haw² jair³	ho² chieh³
comrade	同伴	toong² bahn⁴	t'ung² pan⁴
concern (v)	關於	gwan¹ yeu²	kuan¹ yü²
concert	音樂會	yin¹ yew-eh³ whay⁴	yin¹ yüeh³ hui⁴
concrete	結實	jair² shir²	chieh² shih²
condemn	定罪	ding⁴ dsoo-ee⁴	ting⁴ tsui⁴
conduct	行為	shing² way²	hsing² wei²
confide	信任	shin² run⁴	hsin² jên⁴
confident	自信	tze⁴ shin¹	tzǔ⁴ hsin¹
confront	相對	she-ong¹ doo-ee⁴	hsiang¹ tui⁴
Confucius	孔夫子	koong³ foo¹ tze³	k'ung³ fu¹ tzǔ³
confuse	迷亂	mee² lu-wan⁴	mi² luan⁴
confusion	混亂	hoo-n¹ lu-wan⁴	hun¹ luan⁴
congeal	結冰	jair² bing¹	chieh² ping¹
congress	國會	gwor² whay⁴	kuo² hui⁴
congressman	國會員	gwor² whay⁴ yew-en²	kuo² hui⁴ yüan²
connect	連接	le-en² jair²	lien² chieh²
connection	關係	gwan¹ she⁴	kuan¹ hsi⁴
conquer	征服	jung¹ foo²	chêng¹ fu²
conqueror	征服者	jung¹ foo² jaw³	chêng¹ fu² chê³

	Chinese	Approximation	Wade
conscience	良心	le-ong² shin¹	liang² hsin¹
conscientious	用心	yoong⁴shin¹	yung⁴hsin¹
consent (n)	同意	toong² ee⁴	t'ung² i⁴
consent (v)	同意	toong²ee⁴	t'ung² i⁴
consequence	結果	jair² gwor³	chieh² kuo³
consequently	所以	saw² ee³	so² i³
consider	想以為	she-ong³; ee³ way²	hsiang³; i³ wei²
consideration	致慮	kaow³ leu⁴	k'ao³ lü⁴
consign	交付	je-aow¹ foo⁴	chiao¹ fu⁴
consignee	被交付者	bay⁴je-aow¹ foo⁴ jaw³	pei⁴chiao¹ fu⁴ chê³
consignor	交付者	je-aow¹ foo⁴ jaw³	chiao¹ fu⁴chê³
constant	常	chong²	ch'ang²
consul	領事	ling³ shir¹	ling³ shih¹
consulate	領事館	ling³ shir¹ gwan³	ling³ shih¹ kuan³
contagion	傳染	chwon² rahn³	ch'uan² jan³
contagious	傳染的	chwon² rahn³ dee¹	ch'uan² jan³ ti¹
contain	容	yoong²	jung²
contemporary	同時	toong² shir²	t'ung² shih²
contest (n)	競賽	jing⁴ sy⁴	ching⁴sai⁴
contest (v)	爭論	jung¹ loo-n⁴	chêng¹ lun⁴
continent	大陸	dah⁴ loo⁴	ta⁴lu⁴

49

	Chinese	Approximation	Wade
continual	不斷的	boo¹ dwan⁴ dee¹	pu¹ tuan⁴ ti¹
continue	繼續	jee⁴ sheu⁴	chi⁴ hsü⁴
contract	合同	haw² toong²	ho² t'ung²
contradict	反對	fahn³ doo-ee⁴	fan³ tui⁴
contradiction	矛盾	maow² doo-n⁴	mao² tun⁴
contrary	相反	she-ong¹ fahn²	hsiang¹ fan²
contribute	捐助	jew-en¹ joo²	chüan¹ chu²
control	管理	gwan³ lee³	kuan³ li³
convenience	便利	be-en⁴ lee³	pien⁴ li³
convenient	方便	fong¹ be-en⁴	fang¹ pien⁴
conversation	談話	tahn² whah⁴	t'an² hua⁴
converse	談話	tahn² whah⁴	t'an² hua⁴
convey	運送	yew-n⁴ soong⁴	yün⁴ sung⁴
conveyance	運輸	yew-n⁴ shoo¹	yün⁴ shu¹
cook (n)	廚子	choo² tze³	ch'u² tzŭ³
cook (v)	煮	joo¹	chu¹
cool (adj)	涼的	le-ong² dee¹	liang² ti¹
cool (v)	使涼	shir³ le-ong²	shih³ liang²
cooperate	合作	haw² dsaw⁴	ho² tso⁴
cooperation	合作	haw² dsaw⁴	ho² tso⁴
copper	銅	toong²	t'ung²

	Chinese	Approximation	Wade
copyright	版權	bahn³ chew-en²	pan³ ch'üan²
core	中心	joong¹ shin¹	chung¹ hsin¹
corn	玉米	yeu⁴ mee³·	yü⁴ mi³
corner	角	je-aow²	chiao²
corporate	組合	dsoo³ haw²	tsu³ ho²
corporal	伍長	woo³ chong³	wu³ ch'ang³
corpse	屍	shir¹	shih¹
correct (adj)	對	doo-ee⁴	tui⁴
correct (v)	改正	guy³ jung⁴	kai³ chêng⁴
corrupt (adj)	腐敗	foo³ by⁴	fu³ pai⁴
corrupt (v)	使腐敗	shir² foo³ by⁴	shih² fu³ pai⁴
corruption	腐敗	foo³ by⁴	fu³ pai⁴
cost (n)	價錢	jar³ chen²	chia³ ch'ien²
cost (v)	值	jir²	chih²
costly	貴	gway⁴	kuei⁴
cot	小牀	she-aow³ chwong³	hsiao³ ch'uang³
cotton	棉花	me-en² whah¹	mien² hua¹
cottonseed	棉子	me-en² tze³	mien² tzŭ³
couch	牀榻	chwong;² tah²	ch'uang;² t'a²
cough (n)	咳嗽	cur² saw⁴	k'o² so⁴
cough (v)	咳嗽	cur² saw⁴	k'o² so⁴

	Chinese	Approximation	Wade
count (v)	數算	shoo³; swon¹	shu³; suan¹
counterfeit	假冒	jar³ maow⁴	chia³ mao⁴
country	國鄉下	gwor²; she-ong¹ shah⁴	kuo²; hsiang¹ hsia⁴
couple (n)	一雙一對	ee² shwong'; ee² doo-ee⁴	i² shuang'; i² tui⁴
course	行程	shing² chung²	hsing² ch'êng²
course (study)	課	cur¹	k'o¹
court	天井	te-en¹ jing³	t'ien¹ ching³
courtmartial	軍法	jew-en¹ fah²	chüen¹ fa²
courteous	有禮貌	yoo³ lee³ maow⁴	yu³ li³ mao⁴
courtesy	禮貌	lee³ maow⁴	li³ mao⁴
cousin	表親	be-aow³ chin'	piao³ ch'in'
cover (n)	蓋	guy⁴	kai⁴
cover (v)	掩蓋	yen³ guy⁴	yen³ kai⁴
cow	母牛	moo³ nee-u²	mu³ niu²
coward	膽小的	dahn³ she-aow³ dee'	tan³ hsiao³ ti'
crab	蟹	she-eh⁴	hsieh⁴
cranium	腦殼	naow³ cur²	nao³ k'o²
crawl	爬行	pah² shing²	p'a² hsing²
crazy	瘋狂	fung¹ kwong²	fêng¹ k'uang²

	Chinese	Approximation	Wade

English	Chinese	Approximation	Wade
cream	奶油	ny³ yoo²	nai³ yu²
credible	可信的	cur³ shin¹ dee¹	k'o³ hsin¹ ti¹
credit	信用	shin¹ yoong⁴	hsin¹ yung⁴
creditor	債主	jy⁴ joo³	chai⁴ chu³
credulous	輕信的	ching¹ shin⁴ dee¹	ch'ing¹ hsin⁴ ti¹
crew	船員	chwon² yew-en²	ch'uan² yüan²
crime	罪	dsoo-ee⁴	tsui⁴
criminal	犯人	fahn⁴ run²	fan⁴ jên²
crisis	難關	nahn² gwan¹	nan² kuan¹
crook	騙子	pe-en⁴ tze³	p'ien⁴ tzŭ³
crooked	彎; 不直	wahn¹; boo¹ jir²	wan¹; pu¹ chih²
crop	收成	sho¹ chung²	shou¹ ch'êng²
cross	十字	shir² tze⁴	shih² tzŭ⁴
crow	老鴉	laow³ yah¹	lao³ ya¹
crowd	人羣	run² chew-n²	jên² ch'ün²
crowded	擁擠	yoong³ jee³	yung³ chi³
cruise	巡遊	shew-en² yoo²	hsün² yu²
cruiser	巡洋艦	shew-en² yahng² chen⁴	hsün² yang² ch'ien⁴
cry	叫, 哭, 呼號	je-aow¹; koo¹; hoo haow⁴	chiao¹; k'u¹; hu hao⁴
cucumber	黃瓜	whong² gwah¹	huang² kua¹
cultivate	耕種	gung¹ joong⁴	kêng¹ chung⁴

	Chinese	Approximation	Wade
cultivation	耕種	gung¹ joong⁴	kêng¹ chung⁴
culture	文化	wun² whah⁴	wan² hua⁴
cultured	博學	baw⁴ shoo-er²	po⁴ hsüeh²
cumbersome	笨重	bun⁴ joong⁴	pên⁴ chung⁴
cunning	巧奸詐	che-aow³; je-en¹ jar⁴	ch'iao³; chien¹ cha⁴
cup	茶杯	chah³ bay¹	ch'a³ pei¹
cupboard	碗碟櫃子	wan³ de-air² gway⁴ tze³	wan³ tieh² kuei⁴ tzŭ³
cure	治好	jir⁴ haow³	chih⁴ hao³
curious	好奇	haow⁴ chee²	hao⁴ ch'i²
curtain	簾子帳子	le-en² tzg³; jong⁴ tze³	lien² tzŭ³; chang⁴ tzŭ³
cushion	墊子	de-en⁴ tze²	tien⁴ tzŭ²
custom	風俗	fung¹ soo²	fêng¹ su²
custom (duty)	稅項	shway⁴ she-ong⁴	shui⁴ hsiang⁴
custom house	稅關	shway⁴ gwan⁴	shui⁴ kuan⁴
customary	照例	jaow⁴ lee⁴	chao⁴ li⁴
customer	顧客	goo⁴ cur⁴	ku⁴ k'o⁴
cut (n)	傷	shong¹	shang¹
cut (v)	割切	gur¹; chair²	ko¹; ch'ieh²
cypress	柏樹	baw⁴ shoo⁴	po⁴ shu⁴
D			
daddy	父爹爹	foo¹; de-air¹ de-air¹	fu¹; tieh¹ tieh¹

	Chinese	Approximation	Wade
daily	天天,每日	te-en' te-en' may³ jih⁴	t'ien' t'ien; mei³ jih⁴
damp	潮濕	chaow²shir'	ch'ao² shih'
dance (n)	跳舞	te-aow⁴woo³	t'iao⁴wu³
dance (v)	跳舞	te-aow⁴woo³	t'iao⁴wu³
danger	危險	way² she-en³	wei² hsien³
dangerous	危險的	way² she-en³ dee'	wei² hsien³ ti'
dare	敢	gahn³	kan³
daring	勇敢	yoong² gahn³	yung²kan³
dark	黑暗	hay' ahn⁴	hei' an⁴
darkness	黑暗	hay' ahn⁴	hei' an⁴
date	日期	rih⁴chee'	jih⁴ch'i'
daughter	女兒	neu³ er²	nü³ êrh²
daughter-in-law	媳婦	she² foo⁴	hsi² fu⁴
dawn	天明,天亮	te-en' ming; te-en' le-ong⁴	t'ien' ming; t'ien' liang⁴
day	天,日	te-en; rih⁴	t'ien; jih⁴
daylight	陽光	yahng² gwong'	yang²kuang'
daytime	白天	by² te-en'	pai² t'ien'
dead	死了,亡	sze³ le-aow; wong²	ssŭ³ liao; wang²
deaf	聾	loong²	lung²
dear	親愛	chin' ai⁴	ch'in' ai⁴
death	死,亡	sze; wong²	ssŭ³; wang²

	Chinese	Approximation	Wade
debate (n)	辯論	be-en⁴ loo-n⁴	pien⁴ lun⁴
debate (v)	辯論	be-en⁴ loo-n⁴	pien⁴ lun⁴
debt	債	jy⁴	chai⁴
debtor	債務人	jy⁴ woo⁴ run²	chai⁴ wu⁴ jên²
decapitate	斬	jahn³	chan³
decay (n)	衰落	shwy¹ law⁴	shuai¹ lo⁴
decay (v)	腐爛	foo³ lahn⁴	fu³ lan⁴
decayed	腐爛的	foo³ lahn⁴ dee¹	fu³ lan⁴ ti¹
deceitful	欺騙的	chee¹ pe-en⁴ dee¹	ch'i¹ p'ien⁴ ti¹
deceive	欺騙	chee¹ pe-en⁴	ch'i¹ p'ien⁴
December	十二月	shir² er⁴ yew-eh⁴	shih² êrh⁴ yüeh⁴
decide	定	ding⁴	ting⁴
deck	艙面	tsong¹ me-en⁴	ts'ang¹ mien⁴
decline	向下	she-ong⁴ shah⁴	hsiang⁴ hsia⁴
decrease	減少	je-en² shaow³	chien² shao³
deep	深	shun¹	shên¹
defeat (n)	失敗	shir² by⁴	shih² pai⁴
defeat (v)	打敗	dah³ by⁴	ta³ pai⁴
defect	缺點	chew-eh¹ de-en³	ch'üeh¹ tien³
defense	防護	foong² hoo⁴	fang² hu⁴
defend	保護	baow³ hoo⁴	pao³ hu⁴

	Chinese	Approximation	Wade
deficient	缺	chew-eh¹	ch'üeh¹
degenerate	退化	too-ee⁴ whah⁴	t'ui⁴hua⁴
degeneration	退化	too-ee⁴ whah⁴	t'ui⁴hua⁴
degree	等第,程度	dung³ dee⁴; chung² doo⁴	têng³ ti⁴; ch'êng² tu⁴
deity	神	shun²	shên²
delay (n)	延期	yen² chir²	yen²ch'ih²
delay (v)	延期	yen² chir²	yen²ch'ih²
delicacy	美味	may³ way⁴	mei³ wei⁴
delicate	美味的,細巧的	may³ way⁴dee'; she⁴che-aow³ dee'	mei³ wei⁴ti'; hsi⁴ch'iao³ ti'
delicious	好吃	haow³ chir⁴	hao³ chih⁴
delight (n)	歡喜	whon' she³	huan' hsi³
delight (v)	使歡喜	shir³ whon' she³	shih³ huan' hsi³
deliver	送,寄,交	soong⁴; jee⁴; jo-aow'	sung⁴; chi⁴; chiao'
deliverance	救,釋,放	je-oo⁴; shir² fong⁴	chiu⁴; shih² fang⁴
delude	欺,迷惑	chee'; mee² hwor²	ch'i'; mi²huo²
delusion	迷惑	mee² hwor²	mi² huo²
demand (n)	要求	yaow' che-oo²	yao' oh' iu²
demand (v)	要求	yaow' che-oo²	yao' ch' iu²
democracy	民主國	min² joo³ gwor²	min² chu³ kuo²
democrat	民主黨員	min² joo³ dong³ yew-en²	min² chu³ tang³ yüan²
demote	降級	je-ong⁴jee²	chiang⁴chi²

	Chinese	Approximation	Wade
dense	密	mee^4	mi^4
dentist	牙醫	yah^{2}ee^1	ya^2 i^1
denial	否認	foh^3 run^4	fou^3 jên^4
deny	不認	boo^2 run^4	pu^2 jên^4
depart	離去	lee^2; cheu^4	li^2; ch'ü^4
departure	離去	lee^2 cheu^4	li^2 ch'ü^4
depend	依靠	ee^1 kaow^4	i^1 k'ao^4
deposit (n)	存欵	tsoo-n^{2}kwan^3	ts'un^2 k'uan^3
deposit (v)	存	tsoo-n^2	ts'un^2
depot	棧房,車站	jahn^{4}fong^2; chair^1 jahn^4	chan^4 fang^2; ch'ê^1 chan^4
descend	下	shah^4	hsia^4
descent	下降	shah^4 jeong^4	hsia^4 chiang^4
describe	描寫	me-aow^{2}she-eh^3	miao^2 hsieh^3
description	描寫	me-aow^{2}she-eh^3	miao^2 hsieh^3
desert	沙漠	shah^1 maw^4	sha^1 mo^4
deserter	離棄的	lee^2 chee^{4}dee^1	li^2 ch'i^4 ti^1
design (n)	計畫,圖樣	jee^{4}whah^1; too^2 yong^4	chi^4 hua^1; t'u^2 yang^4
design (v)	設計	sher^{4}jee^4	shê^4 chi^4
desire (n)	慾望	yeu^{4}wong^4	yü^4 wang^4
desire (v)	要,欲,想	yaow^4; yoo^4; she-ong^3	yao^4; yu^4; hsiang^3
desk	書桌	shoo^1 jaw^1	shu^1 cho^1

	Chinese	Approximation	Wade
desolate	荒涼	whong¹ le-ong²	huang¹ liang²
despair	絕望	jew-eh² wong⁴	chüeh² wang⁴
destination	目的地	moo⁴ dee¹ dee⁴	mu⁴ ti¹ ti⁴
destiny	命運	ming⁴ yew-an⁴	ming⁴ yün⁴
destroy	毀壞	whay³ why⁴	hui³ huai⁴
destruction	破壞	paw⁴ why⁴	p'o⁴ huai⁴
detach	分開	fun¹ ky¹	fên¹ k'ai¹
detain	拘留	jeu¹ le-oo²	chü¹ liu²
determination	決斷	jew-eh² doo-an⁴	chüeh² tuan⁴
determine	定	ding⁴	ting⁴
develop	長成	jong³ chung²	chang³ ch'êng²
device	方法	fong¹ fah³	fang¹ fa³
devil	鬼	gway³	kuei³
devote	熱心	raw¹ shin¹	jo¹ hsin¹
devotion	專誠	jwon¹ chung²	chuan¹ chêng²
dew	露水	loo⁴ shway³	lu⁴ shui³
dialect	方言	fong¹ yen²	fang¹ yen²
diary	日記	rih⁴ jee⁴	jih⁴ chi⁴
die	死	sze³	ssŭ³
differ	不同	boo¹ toong²	pu¹ t'ung²
difference	差別	chah¹ be-air²	ch'a¹ pieh²

	Chinese	Approximation	Wade
different	差, 不同	chah; boo toong²	ch'a; pu t'ung²
difficult	難	nahn	nan
digest	消化	she-aow whah⁴	hsiao hua⁴
digestion	消化力	she-aow whah⁴ lee⁴	hsiao hua⁴ li⁴
dignified	莊嚴	jwong yen²	chuang yen
dignity	威儀	way ee²	wei i²
dim	瞇糊	mee hoo²	mi² hu
dime	一毫	ee haow²	i hao²
dine	吃飯	chir fahn⁴	ch'ih fan⁴
dinner	晚飯	wan³ fahn⁴	wan³ fan⁴
direct (adj)	直接	jir² jair	chih² chieh
direct (v*	囑咐	joo³ foo⁴	chu³ fu⁴
direction	方向	fong she-ong⁴	fang hsiang⁴
dirt	泥土	nee too³	ni t'u³
dirty	骯髒	ahng dsong	ang tsang
disagree	不同意	boo toong ee⁴	pu t'ung i⁴
disagreement	爭端	jung dwon	chêng tuan
disappear	消滅	she-aow me-air⁴	hsiao mieh⁴
disappearance	失踪	shir dsoong²	shih tsung²
disappointed	失望	shir wong⁴	shih wang⁴
disarmament	解兵	jair³ bing	chieh³ ping

	Chinese	Approximation	Wade
disaster	災禍	dsy' hwor^4	tsai' huo^4
disastrous	不幸	boo' shing^4	pu' hsing^4
disciple	徒弟	too^2 dee^4	t'u^2 ti^4
discipline	紀律	jee^4 leu^4	chi^4 lü^4
discourage	使失意	shir^3 shir' ee^4	shih^3 shih' i^4
discount (n)	折扣	jaw^2 koh^4	chê^2 k'ou^4
discount (v)	打折扣	dah^3 jaw^2 koh^4	ta^3 chê^2 k'ou^4
discover	發現	fah' she-en^4	fa' hsien^4
discriminate	分別	fun' be-air^2	fên' pieh^2
discrimination	區別	cheu' be-air^2	ch'ü' pieh^2
discuss	討論	taow^3 loo-n^4	t'ao^3 lun^4
disease	病	bing^4	ping^4
diseased	有病	yoo^3 bing^4	yu^3 ping^4
disgrace	恥辱	jir^3 roo^4	chih^3 ju^4
disgraceful	無恥	woo^2 jir^3	wu^2 chih^3
dish	碟子	te-air^2 tze^3	tieh^2 tzǔ^3
dishonest	不誠實	boo' jung^2 shir^2	pu' chêng^2 shih^2
dislike	嫌	she-en^2	hsien^2
dismiss	開除	ky' choo^2	k'ai' ch'u^2
dismount	下馬	shah^4 mah^3	hsia^4 ma^3
disobey	違背	way' bay^4	wei' pei^4

	Chinese	Approximation	Wade
disorder	紛亂	fun¹ loo-an⁴	fên¹ luan⁴
dispatch	電信	de-en⁴ shen⁴	tien⁴ hsin⁴
disperse	解散	jair³ sahn⁴	chieh³ san⁴
displeased	不喜歡	boo¹ she³ whon¹	pu¹ hsi³ huan¹
dispose	安排	ahn¹ py²	an¹ p'ai²
disposition	本性	bun³ shing⁴	pên³ hsing⁴
dispute (n)	爭論	jung¹ loo-n²	chêng¹ lun²
dispute (v)	分爭	fun¹ jung¹	fên¹ chêng¹
disqualify	不合格	boo¹ haw² gur²	pu¹ ho² ko²
disregard	不顧	boo¹ goo⁴	pu¹ ku⁴
disrespect	失敬	shir¹ jing⁴	shih¹ ching⁴
dissatisfaction	不滿意	boo¹ mahn³ ee⁴	pu¹ man³ i⁴
dissimilar	異同	ee⁴ toong²	i⁴ t'ung²
dissolve	消	she-aow¹	hsiao¹
distance	距離	jeu⁴ lee²	chü⁴ li²
distant	遠	yew-an²	yüan²
distinct	清楚	ching¹ choo³	ch'ing¹ ch'u³
distinguished	非常	fay¹ chong²	fei¹ ch'ang²
distress	苦痛	koo³ toong⁴	k'u³ t'ung⁴
distribute	分配	fun¹ pay⁴	fên¹ p'ei⁴
distribution	配置	pay⁴ jir⁴	p'ei⁴ chih⁴

	Chinese	Approximation	Wade
district	區域	cheu¹ yeu⁴	ch'ü¹ yü⁴
distrust	不信任	boo¹ shin⁴ run⁴	pu¹ hsin⁴ jên⁴
disturb	鬧事	naow⁴ shir¹	nao⁴ shih¹
ditch	溝	goh¹	kou¹
dive	跳入水	te-aow⁴ roo⁴ shway³	t'iao⁴ ju⁴ shui³
divide	分	fun¹	fên¹
dividend	股息	goo³ she²	ku³ hsi²
divine	神	shun²	shên²
divinity	神性	shun² shing⁴	shên² hsing⁴
divorce	離婚	lee² hoo-n¹	li² hun¹
do	做	dsaw⁴	tso⁴
doctor	醫生	ee¹ shung¹	i¹ shêng¹
doctrine	理論	lee³ loo-n⁴	li³ lun⁴
dog	狗	goh³	kou³
dollar	洋錢	yong² chen²	yang² ch'ien²
domestic	家務	jar¹ woo⁴	chia¹ wu⁴
done	做完	dsaw⁴ wan²	tso⁴ wan²
donkey	驢	leu²	lü²
don't	不可	boo¹ cur³	pu¹ k'o³
door	門戶	mun; hoo⁴	mên; hu⁴
dot	一點	ee⁴ de-en³	i⁴ tien³

	Chinese	Approximation	Wade
double (n)	一 雙	ee¹ shwong¹	i¹ shuang¹
double (v)	成 雙	chung² shwong¹	ch'êng² shuang¹
doubt (n)	疑 惑	ee² hwor⁴	i² huo⁴
doubt (v)	起 疑	chee³ ee²	ch'i³ i²
dove	鴿 子	gur¹ tze³	ko¹ tzŭ³
down	下	shah⁴	hsia⁴
downstairs	樓 下	loh² shah⁴	lou² hsia⁴
dozen	一 打	ee⁴ dah³	i⁴ ta³
dragon	龍	loong²	lung²
drain (n)	溝 道	goh¹ daow⁴	kou¹ tao⁴
drain (v)	瀉 下	she-eh⁴ shah⁴	hsieh⁴ hsia⁴
drawer	抽 屜	choh¹ dee⁴	ch'ou¹ ti⁴
drawing	畫	whah⁴	hua⁴
dread	怕	pah⁴	p'a⁴
dreadful	可 怕	cur³ pah⁴	k'o³ p'a⁴
dream (n)	夢	mung⁴	mêng⁴
dream (v)	做 夢	dsaw⁴ mung⁴	tso⁴ mêng⁴
dregs	渣 子	jah¹ tze³	cha¹ tzŭ³
dress (n)	衣 服	ee¹ foo²	i¹ fu²
dress (v)	穿 衣	chwon¹ ee¹	ch'uan¹ i¹
drill	體 操	tee³ tsaow¹	t'i³ ts'ao¹

English	Chinese	Approximation	Wade
drink	喝	haw¹	ho¹
drive	趕	gahn³	kan³
driver	趕車的	gahn³ jaw¹ dee¹	kan³ chê¹ ti¹
drown	淹死	yan¹ sze³	yen¹ ssŭ³
dry (adj)	乾	gahn¹	kan¹
dry (v)	曬乾	shy⁴ gahn¹	shai⁴ kan¹
duck.	鴨子	yah¹ tze³	ya¹ tzŭ³
dull	愚笨	yeu² bun⁴	yŭ² pên⁴
dumb	啞	yah³	ya³
dung	糞	fun⁴	fên⁴
dust	塵土	chun² too³	chên² t'u³
duty	本分, 責任	bun³ fun¹; dseh² run⁴	pên³ fên¹; tsê² jên⁴
dwell	住	joo⁴	chu⁴
dwelling	住宅	joo⁴ jy²	chu⁴ chai²
dye (n)	染料	rahn³ le-aow⁴	jan³ liao⁴
dye (v)	染	rahn³	jan³
dyke	堤	dee¹	ti¹
dynamite	炸藥	jah⁴ yaow⁴	cha⁴ yao⁴
dynasty	朝代	chaow² dy⁴	ch'ao² tai⁴
dysentery	痢疾	lee⁴ jee²	li⁴ chi²
each	每	may³	mei³

	Chinese	Approximation	Wade
edit	編輯	be-en¹ jee⁴	pien¹ chi⁴
educate	教	je-aow⁴	chiao⁴
education	教育	je-aow⁴ yeu⁴	chiao⁴ yü⁴
eel	鱔魚	shahn⁴ yeu²	shan⁴ yü²
effect (n)	效力	she-aow⁴ lee⁴	hsiao⁴ li⁴
effect (to give)	執行	jir² shing²	chih² hsing²
effort	努力	noo³ lee⁴	nu³ li⁴
egg	鷄蛋	jee¹ dahn⁴	chi¹ tan⁴
egoism	主我主義	joo² woh² joo³ ee⁴	chu² wo² chu³ i⁴
elated	高興	gaow¹ shing⁴	kao¹ hsing⁴
elder	長者	jong³ jaw³	chang³ chê³
eldest	最長	dsway⁴ jong³	tsui⁴ chang³
elected	當選	dong¹ shew-en³	tang¹ hsüan³
election	選擧	shew-en³ jeu³	hsüan³ chü³
electricity	電氣	de-en⁴ chee	tien⁴ ch'i⁴
electric light	電燈	de-en⁴ dung¹	tien⁴ têng¹
electric power	電力	de-en⁴ lee⁴	tien⁴ li⁴
elegant	高雅	gaow¹ yah³	kao¹ ya³
elementary	初步	choo¹ boo⁴	ch'u¹ pu⁴
elephant	象	she-ong⁴	hsiang⁴
else	別的,另外	be-air² dee; ling² wy⁴	pieh¹ ti; ling² wai⁴

	Chinese	Approximation	Wade
elucidate	說明	shoo-aw¹ ming²	shuo¹ ming²
embark	上船	shong² chwon²	shang² ch'uan²
embassy	大使館	dah⁴ shir³ gwon³	ta⁴ shih³ kuan³
embrace (include)	包括	baow¹ gwah⁴	pao¹ kua⁴
embrace (fold in arms)	抱, 摟	baow⁴; loh³	pao⁴; lou³
eminent	高明	gaow¹ ming²	kao¹ ming²
empire	帝國	dee⁴ gwor²	ti⁴ kuo²
employ	使, 用	shir³; yoong⁴	shih³; yung⁴
employment	事業	shir⁴ yair⁴	shih⁴ yeh⁴
empty	空的	koong¹ dee¹	k'ung¹ ti¹
encounter	相逢	she-ong¹ fung²	hsiang¹ fêng²
encourage	勉勵	me-en³ lee⁴	mien³ li⁴
end (aim)	目的	moo⁴ dee¹	mu⁴ ti¹
end (v)	終結	joong¹ jair²	chung¹ chieh²
endless	無窮	woo² che-oong²	wu² ch'iung²
endurance	忍耐力	run³ ny⁴ lee⁴	jên³ nai⁴ li⁴
endure	忍耐	run³ ny⁴	jên³ nai⁴
enemy	敵人	dee² run²	ti² jên²
engage	請聘	ching³; pin⁴	ch'ing³; p'in⁴
engagement	約會	yew-eh¹ whay⁴	yüeh¹ hui⁴
engineer	工程師	goong¹ chung² shir¹	kung¹ ch'êng² shih¹

	Chinese	Approximation	Wade
English	英國的	ying¹ gwor² dee˙	ying¹ kuo² ti¹
English (language)	英文	ying¹ wun²	ying¹ wên²
enjoy	取樂	cheu³ loh⁴	ch'ü³ lo⁴
enlarge	擴大	kwong⁴ dah	k'uang⁴ ta⁴
enough	足夠	dsoo² goh⁴	tsu² kou⁴
enter	入進	roo; jin⁴	ju; chin⁴
entire	完全	wan² jew-en²	wan² chüan²
enumerate	計算	jee⁴ swon⁴	chi⁴ suan⁴
envelop	信封	shin⁴ fung¹	hsin⁴ fêng¹
envoy	專使	jwon¹ shir³	chuan¹ shih³
epidemic	流行病	lee-oo² shing² bing⁴	liu² hsing² ping⁴
epoch	時代	shir² dy⁴	shih² tai⁴
equality	平等	ping² dung³	p'ing² têng³
era	紀元	jee⁴ yew-en²	chi⁴ yüan²
erase	擦去	tsah cheu⁴	ts'a ch'ü⁴
erect	建立	je-en⁴ lee⁴	chien⁴ li⁴
err	作錯	dsaw⁴ tsaw⁴	tso⁴ ts'o⁴
errand	差事	chy¹ shir⁴	ch'ai¹ shih⁴
error	錯誤	tsaw⁴ woo⁴	ts'o⁴ wu⁴
escape	脫逃	taw¹ taow²	t'o¹ t'ao²
escort (n)	護送	hoo⁴ soong⁴	hu⁴ sung⁴

	Chinese	Approximation	Wade
escort (v)	押解	yah^1 jair^4	ya^1 chieh^4
essence	精	jing^1	ching^1
essential	必要的	bee^2 yaow^4 dee^1	pi^2 yao^4 ti^1
establish	設立	sheh^4 lee^4	shê^4 li^4
estate	家產	jar^1 chahn^3	chia^1 ch'an^3
esteem	敬重	jing^4 joong^4	ching^4 chung^4
estimate (n)	估價	goo^1 jar^1	ku^1 chia^1
estimate (v)	計算	jee^4 swon^4	chi^4 suan^4
estrange	離間 疏遠	lee^2 je-en;^{4} soo^1 yew-en^3	li^2 chien;^{4} su^1 yüan^3
eternal	永久	yoong^3 jee-oo^3	yung^3 chiu^3
eternity	永遠	yoong^3 yew-en^3	yung^3 yüan^3
ethics	倫理學	loo-n^2 lee^3 shoo-er^2	lun^2 li^3 hsüeh^2
etiquette	禮儀	lee^3 ee^1	li^3 i^1
eulogy	誇贊	kwah^1 dsahn^4	k'ua^1 tsan^4
Europe	歐洲	oh^1 joh^1	ou^1 chou^1
European	歐洲的	oh^1 joh^1 dee^1	ou^1 chou^1 ti^1
even	平	ping^2	p'ing^2
evening	晚上	wan^3 shong^4	wan^3 shang^4
eventual	早晚	dsaow^3 wan^3	tsao^3 wan^3
every	每,各	may;^{3} gur^4	mei;^{3} ko^4
every-day	每天	may^3 te-en^1	mei^3 t'ien^1

	Chinese	Approximation	Wade
everywhere	到 處	daow⁴ choo³	tao⁴ ch'u³
evil	惡	aw³	o³
evolution	進 化	jin⁴ whah⁴	chin⁴ hua⁴
exact	準 確	joo-n³ chew-eh⁴	chun³ ch'üeh⁴
examination	考 試	kaow³ shir⁴	k'ao³ shih⁴
examine	檢 查	je-en³ chah²	chien³ ch'a²
exceed	超 過	chaow' gwor⁴	ch'ao' kuo⁴
excellent	最 好	dsway⁴ haow³	tsui⁴ hao³
exception	倒 外	lee⁴ wy⁴	li⁴ wai⁴
exceptional	非 常	fay' chong²	fei' ch'ang²
excessive	太 過	ty⁴ gwor⁴	t'ai⁴ kuo⁴
exchange (n)	交 易	je-aow' oo	chiao' i⁴
exchange (v)	交 換	je-aow' whan⁴	chiao' huan⁴
excite	煽 惑	shahn⁴ hwor⁴	shan⁴ huo⁴
excitement	哄 動	hoong' doong⁴	hung' tung⁴
exclude	除 去	choo² cheu⁴	ch'u² ch'ü⁴
exclusive	專 用	jwon' yoong⁴	chuan' yung⁴
exercise (n)	運 動	yew-n⁴ doong⁴	yün⁴ tung⁴
exercise	課 程	cur⁴ chung²	k'o⁴ ch'êng²
exert	盡 力	jin⁴ lee⁴	chin⁴ li⁴
exhaust	用 盡	yoong⁴ jin⁴	yung⁴ chin⁴

	Chinese	Approximation	Wade
exhausted	精疲	jing¹ pee²	ching¹ p'i²
exhibit	陳列	jun² le-eh⁴	chên² lieh⁴
exhibition	展覽會	jahn³ lahn³ whay⁴	chan³ lan³ hui⁴
existence	生活	shung¹ hwor²	shêng¹ huo²
expand	伸張	shun¹ jong¹	shên¹ chang¹
expect	盼望	pahn⁴ wong⁴	p'an⁴ wang⁴
expel	驅逐	cheu joo⁴	ch'ü chu⁴
expenditure	費用	fay⁴ yoong⁴	fei⁴ yung⁴
expensive	貴	gway⁴	kuei⁴
experience	經驗	jing¹ yen⁴	ching¹ yen⁴
experiment	試驗	shir⁴ yen⁴	shih⁴ yen⁴
expert	專家	jwon⁴ jar¹	chuan⁴ chia¹
export	出口	choo¹ koh³	ch'u¹ k'ou³
express	表示	be-aow³ shir⁴	piao³ shih⁴
extend	擴充	kwor⁴ choong¹	k'uo⁴ ch'ung¹
extensive	寬大	kwon¹ dah¹	k'uan¹ ta¹
external	外面	wy⁴ me-en⁴	wai⁴ mien⁴
extraordinary	非凡	fay¹ fahn²	fei¹ fan²
extreme	極端	jee² dwon¹	chi² tuan¹
extremity	極處	jee² cheu⁴	chi² ch'ü⁴
eye	眼睛	yen³ jing¹	yen³ ching¹

	Chinese	Approximation	Wade
eyeball	眼珠	yen³ joo`	yen³ chu`
eyebrow	眉毛	may² maow²	mei² mao²
eye-pupil	瞳人	toong² run²	t'ung² jên²
eyesight	眼力	yen³ lee⁺	yen³ li⁺
eye-witness	証人	jung⁺ run²	chêng⁺ jên²

F

face (n)	面部	me-en⁺ boo⁺	mien⁺ pu⁺
face (v)	對面	doo-ee⁺ me-en⁺	tui⁺ mien
fact	事實	shir⁺ shir²	shih⁺ shih²
fade	衰落	shwy` loh⁺	shuai` lo⁺
fail	失敗	shir` by⁺	shih` pai⁺
faint	發暈	fah` yew-n"	fa` yün⁺
fairy	神仙	shun² she-en`	shên² hsien`
faith	信仰	shin⁺ yong³	hsin⁺ yang³
faithful	忠實	joong` shir²	chung` shih²
fall	掉下	de-aow⁺ shah⁺	tiao⁺ hsia⁺
false	虛假	sheu` jar³	hsü` chia³
fame	名望	ming² yeu²	ming² yü²
family	家庭	jar` ting`	chia` t'ing`
famous	有名的	yoo³ ming² dee	yu³ ming² ti`
far	遠	yew-en³	yüan³

	Chinese	Approximation	Wade
farewell	再見	dsy⁴ je-en⁴	tsai⁴ chien⁴
farm	田地	te-en² dee⁴	t'ien² ti⁴
farmer	農夫	nung² foo¹	nung² fu¹
fast	快	kwy⁴	k'uai⁴
fat	肥	fay²	fei²
fate	命運	ming⁴ yew-n⁴	ming⁴ yün⁴
father	父親	foo⁴ chin¹	fu⁴ ch'in¹
father-in-law	岳父	yaw⁴ foo⁴	yo⁴ fu⁴
fathom	測量	chee¹ le-ong²	ch'i¹ liang²
fatigue	疲倦	pee² chew-en⁴	p'i² ch'üan⁴
fault	過錯	gwor⁴ tsaw⁴	kuo⁴ ts'o⁴
favor	恩惠	un¹ whay⁴	ên¹ hui⁴
fear (v)	怕	pah⁴	p'a⁴
feast (n)	宴會	yen⁴ whay⁴	yen⁴ hui⁴
February	二月	er⁴ yew-eh⁴	êrh⁴ yüeh⁴
feed	喂	way⁴	wei⁴
feel	覺得	jew-eh² teh²	chüeh² t'ê²
felicity	快樂	kwy⁴ law⁴	k'uai⁴ lo⁴
female	女的, 牝的	neu³ dee¹; moo³ dee¹	nü³ ti¹; mu³ ti¹
ferryboat	渡船	doo⁴ chwon²	tu⁴ ch'uan²
fertile	肥豐	fay²; fung¹	fei²; fêng¹

	Chinese	Approximation	Wade
festival	節	jair^2	chieh^2
fever	發燒	fah^1 shaow^1	fa^1 shao^1
few	少	shaow^3	shao^3
field	田	te-en^2	t'ien^2
field-hospital	戰地病院	jahn^4 dee^4 bing^4 yew-en^4	chan^4 ti^4 ping^4 yüan^4
fifteen	十五	shir^2 woo^3	shih^2 wu^3
fifty	五十	woo^3 shir^2	wu^3 shih^2
fig	無花果	woo^2 whah^1 gwor^3	wu^2 hua^1 kuo^3
fight (n)	戰	jahn^4	chan^4
fight (v)	打架	dah^3 jar^4	ta^3 chia^4
figure	形像	shing^2 she-ong^4	hsing^2 hsiang^4
figure (number)	數目	shoo^4 moo^4	shu^4 mu^4
filial	孝順	she-aow^4 shoo-n^4	hsiao^4 shun^4
fill	充滿	choong^1 mahn^3	ch'ung^1 man^3
film	電影	de-en^4 ying^3	tien^4 ying^3
filthy	污臭	woo^1 choh^4	wu^1 ch'ou^4
final	最後	dsay^4 hoh^4	tsui^4 hou^4
finance	財政	tsy^2 jung^4	ts'ai^2 chêng^4
find	找到	jaow^3 daow^4	chao^3 tao^4
fine (n)	美細	she; may^3	hsi; mei^3
fine (v)	罰	fah^2	fa^2

	Chinese	Approximation	Wade
fine arts	美術	may³ shoo⁴	mei³ shu⁴
finger	指頭	jir² toh²	chih² t'ou²
finish (v)	作完	dsaw⁴ wan²	tso⁴ wan²
finite	有限	yoo³ she-en⁴	yu³ hsien⁴
fire (n)	火	hwor³	huo³
fire (v)	放	fong⁴	fang⁴
firecracker	煙爆	be-en¹ paow⁴	pien¹ p'ao⁴
fireplace	壁爐	bee⁴ loo²	pi⁴ lu²
firewood	柴火	chy² hwor³	ch'ai² huo³
firm	堅穩	je-en¹; wun³	chien¹; wên³
first	第一初	dee⁴ ee; choo¹	ti⁴ i; ch'u¹
fish (n)	魚	yeu²	yü²
fish (v)	釣魚	de-aow⁴ yeu²	tiao⁴ yü²
fisherman	魚翁	yeu² wung¹	yü² wêng¹
fist	拳	chew-en²	ch'üan²
fit	相合	she-ong¹ haw²	hsiang¹ ho²
five	五	woo³	wu³
fix	修理	she-oo¹ lee³	hsiu¹ li³
flag	旗	chee²	ch'i²
flat	平	ping²	p'ing²
flee	逃	taow²	t'ao²

	Chinese	Approximation	Wade
fleet	艦隊	je-en⁴ doo-ee⁴	chien⁴ tui⁴
flesh	肉	roh⁴	jou⁴
float	浮 漂	foo²; pe-aow¹	fu²; p'iao¹
flood	水災	shway³ dsy¹	shui³ tsai¹
floor	地板	dee⁴ bahn³	ti⁴ pan³
flour	麵粉	me-en⁴ fun³	mien⁴ fên³
flow	流	lee-oo²	liu²
flower (n)	花	whah¹	hua¹
flower (v)	開花	ky¹ whah¹	k'ai¹ hua¹
flute	笛子	dee² tze³	ti² tzŭ³
fly (n)	蠅子	ying¹ tze³	ying¹ tzŭ³
fly (v)	飛	fay¹	fei¹
fog	霧	woo⁴	wu⁴
foliage	葉	yair⁴	yeh⁴
follow	隨 從跟	soo-ee² tsoong²; gun¹	sui² ts'ung²; kên¹
follower	門人	mun² run²	mên² jên²
fond of	喜歡	she³ whon¹	hsi³ huan¹
food	食物	shir² woo⁴	shih² wu⁴
fool	傻子	shah³ tze³	sha³ tzŭ³
foolish	糊塗	hoo² doo²	hu² tu²
foot	腳	je-aow³	chiao³

	Chinese	Approximation	Wade
foot (measure)	一尺	ee^{4}chir^3	i^4 ch'ih^3
football	足球	dsoo^{2}chee-oo^2	tsu^{2}ch'iu^2
footstep	腳步	je-aow^{3}boo^4	chiao^3 pu^4
for	為	way^4	wei^4
forbid	禁止	jin^{4}jir^3	chin^{4}chih^3
force (n)	力	lee^4	li^4
force (v)	逼着	be^{4}jaw^4	pi^{4}cho^4
ford	渡河	doo^{4}haw^2	tu^{4}ho^2
forehead	額骨	uh^{2}goo^2	e^{2}ku^2
foreign	外洋	wy; yong^2	wai; yang^2
foreigner	外國人	wy^{4}gwor^{2}run^2	wai^4 kuo^2 jên^2
forenoon	上午	shong^{4}woo^3	shang^{4}wu^3
forest	樹林	shoo^{4}lin^2	shu^{4}lin^2
forget	忘記	wong^{4}jee^4	wang^{4}chi^4
forgive	原諒	yew-en^{4}le-ong^4	yüan^{4}liang^4
forgiveness	饒恕	raow^{2}shoo^4	jao^{2}shu^4
fork	叉子	chah'tze^3	ch'a'tzŭ^3
form	形式	shing^{2}shir^4	hsing^{2}shih^4
formerly	從前	tsoong^{2}che-en^2	ts'ung^{2}ch'ien^2
fortnight	兩星期	le-ong^{2}shing'chee^2	liang^{2}hsing'ch'i^1
foundation	基礎	jee'choo^3	chi'ch'u^3

77

	Chinese	Approximation	Wade
fountain pen	墨水筆	maw^4 shway^3 bee^3	mo^4 shui^3 pi^3
fragrant	香	she-ong^1	hsiang^1
France	法國	fah^2 gwor^4	fa^2 kuo^4
free	自由	tze^4 yoo^2	tzŭ^4 yu^2
freeze	上凍	shang^4 doong^4	shang^4 tung^4
French	法國的	fah^2 gwor^4 dee^2	fa^2 kuo^4 ti^2
Frenchman	法國人	fah^2 gwor^4 run^2	fa^2 kuo^4 jên^2
fresh	新鮮	shin^1 she-en^1	hsin^1 hsien^1
Friday	星期五	shing^1 chee^2 woo^3	hsing^1 ch'i^2 wu^3
friend	朋友	pung^2 yoo^3	pêng^2 yu^3
friendship	交情	je-aow^1 ching^1	chiao^1 ch'ing^1
frighten	嚇	shah^4	hsia^4
frightened	受驚	shoh^4 jing^1	shou^4 ching^1
frog	田雞	te-en^2 jee^1	t'ien^2 chi^1
from	從	tsoong^2	ts'ung^2
front	前面	chen^2 me-en^4	ch'ien^2 mien^4
frontier	邊界	be-en^1 jair^4	pien^1 chieh^4
frost	霜	shwong^1	shuang^1
frugal	儉省	je-en^3 shung^3	chien^3 shêng^3
fruit	水果	shway^3 gwor^3	shui^3 kuo^3
fry	煎炸	je-en^1; chah^2	chien^1; cha^2

	Chinese	Approximation	Wade
fuel	柴火	chy' hwor³	ch'ai' huo³
full	滿	mahn³	man³
function	任務	run' woo⁴	jên⁴ wu⁴
fundamental	根本的	gun' bun³ dee'	kên' pên³ ti'
funds	欵項	kwon³ she-ong⁴	k'uan³ hsiang⁴
funeral	出喪	choo' song'	ch'u' sang'
funny	可笑	cur³ she-aow⁴	k'o³ hsiao⁴
fur	毛	maow²	mao²
future	將來	je-ong' ly²	chiang' lai²
G			
gain	賺	jwon⁴	chuan⁴
gale	大風	dah⁴ fung'	ta⁴ fêng'
gamble	賭錢	doo³ che-en²	tu³ ch'ien²
game	遊戲	yoo² she⁴	yu² hsi⁴
gaol	監獄	je-on' yeu⁴	chien' yü⁴
gap	山口	shahn' koh³	shan' k'ou³
garage	車行	chair' hong²	ch'ê' hang²
garden	花園	whah' yew-en²	hua' yüan²
gardener	花匠	whah' je-ong⁴	hua' chiang⁴
gargle	嗽口	shoo⁴ koh³	shu⁴ k'ou³
gas	氣	chee⁴	ch'i⁴

	Chinese	Approximation	Wade
gasoline	汽油	chee⁺ yew²	ch'i⁴ yu²
gate	大門	dah⁴ mun²	ta⁴ mên²
gather	聚採	jeu⁺ tsy³	chü⁺ ts'ai³
gay	快活	kwy⁺ hwor¹	k'uai⁴ huo²
gaze	望	wong⁴	wang⁴
general (adj)	通常	toong¹ chong¹	t'ung¹ ch'ang²
general (military)	上將	shong⁺ je-ong⁴	shang⁴ chiang⁴
generalissimo	大元帥	dah² yew-en² shwy⁴	ta² yüan² shuai⁴
generally	通例,都	toong¹ lee⁺ doo¹	t'ung¹ li⁴ tu¹
generate	生	shung¹	shêng¹
generation	一代	ee¹ dy⁴	i¹ tai⁴
generous (capacity)	大量	dah⁴ le-ong²	ta⁴ liang²
generous (attribute)	寬仁	kwon¹ run²	k'uan¹ jên²
genius	天才	te-en¹ tsy²	t'ien¹ ts'ai²
gentleman	君子先生	jew-n¹ tze³ she-en¹ shung¹	chün¹ tzŭ³ hsien¹ shêng¹
genuine	真實	jun¹ shir²	chên¹ shih²
geography	地理學	dee⁺ lee³ shoo-er²	ti⁴ li³ hsüeh²
geology	地質學	dee⁴ jir³ shoo-er²	ti⁴ chih³ hsüeh²
German (n)	德國人	deh² gwor² run²	tê² kuo² jên²
German (adj)	德國的	deh² gwor² dee¹	tê² kuo² ti¹
Germany	德國	deh² gwor²	tê² kuo²

	Chinese	Approximation	Wade
get (in)	進來	jin^4 ly^2	chin^4 lai^2
get (out)	出去	choo^1 cheu^3	ch'u^1 ch'ü^3
get (up)	上去	shong^4 cheu^3	shang^4 ch'ü^3
ghost	鬼	gway^3	kuei^3
giant	高人	gaow^1 run^2	kao^1 jên^2
gift	禮物	lee^3 woo^4	li^3 wu^4
gigantic	偉大	way^3 dah^4	wei^3 ta^4
ginger	薑	je-ong^1	chiang^1
girl	女孩子	neu^3 hy^2 tze^3	nü^3 hai^2 tzu^3
gist	大意	dah^4 ee^4	ta^4 i^4
give	給,與	gay; yoo^3	kei; yu^3
give in marriage	出嫁	choo^1 jar^4	ch'u^1 chia^4
glad	喜歡	she^3 whon^1	hsi^3 huan^1
glass	玻璃	baw^1 lee^2	po^1 li^2
glass (tumbler)	玻璃盃	baw^1 lee^2 bay^1	po^1 li^2 pei^1
glasses (eye)	眼鏡	yen^3 jing^4	yen^3 ching^4
globe	地球	dee^4 chee-oo^2	ti^4 ch'iu^2
gloomy	不明亮	boo^4 ming^2 wong^4	pu^4 ming^2 wang^4
glory	光榮	gwong^1 roong^2	kuang^1 jung^2
glove	手套	shoh^3 taow^4	shou^3 t'ao^4
go	到	daow^4	tao^4

	Chinese	Approximation	Wade
go out	出去	choo^1 cheu^3	ch'u^1 ch'ü^3
go up	上去	shong^4 cheu^3	shang^4 ch'ü^3
goat	山羊	shahn^1 yong^2	shan^1 yang^2
God	上帝	shong^4 dee^4	shang^4 ti^4
gold	金子	jin^1 tze^3	chin^1 tzŭ^3
golden	金的	jin^1 dee^1	chin^1 ti^1
gone	去了	cheu^3 law^4	ch'ü^3 lo^4
good	好善良	haow^3; shahn^4; le-ong^2	hao^3; shan^4; liang^2
good-afternoon	好啊	haow^3 ah´	hao^3 ah´
good-evening	好啊	haow^3 ah´	hao^3 ah´
good-morning	您早	neen^2 dsaow^3	nin^2 tsao^3
good-bye	再見	tsy^4 jo-en^4	tsai^4 chien^4
goodness	德行	deh^2 shing^2	tê^2 hsing^4
good-night	明天見	ming^2 te-en^1 je-en^4	ming^2 t'ien^1 chien^4
goods	貨物	hwor^4 woo^4	huo^4 wu^4
gossip	閒談	she-en^2 tahn^2	hsien^2 t'an^2
govern	治理	jir^1 lee^3	chih^1 li^3
governor	總督	dsoong^3 doo^1	tsung^3 tu^1
government	政府	jung^4 foo^3	chêng^4 fu^3
grace	恩惠	un^1 whay^4	ên^1 hui^4
gradation	次第	tze^4 dee^4	tzŭ^4 ti^4

	Chinese		Approximation	Wade
grade	等級		dung^2 jee^2	têng^2 chi^2
graduate	畢業生		bee^4 yair^4 shung^1	pi^4 yeh^4 shêng^1
graduation	畢業		bee^4 yair^4	pi^4 yeh^4
grain	糧食		le-ong^2 shir^2	liang^2 shih^2
grammar	文法		wun^1 fah^3	wên^2 fa^3
grand	偉大		way^2 dah^4	wei^2 ta^4
granddaughter	孫女		soo-n^1 neu^3	sun^1 nü^3
grandfather	祖父		dsoo^3 foo^4	tsu^3 fu^4
grandmother	祖母		dsoo^3 moo^3	tsu^3 mu^3
grandson	孫子		soo-n^1 tze^3	sun^1 tzŭ^3
granite	青石		ching^1 shir^2	ch'ing^1 shih^2
grant	允准		yew-n^3 joo-n^3	yün^3 chun^3
grape	葡萄		poo^2 taow^2	p'u^2 t'ao^2
grasp	拿住		nah^2 joo^4	na^2 chu^4
grass	草		tsaow^3	ts'ao^3
grateful	感激		gahn^3 jee^1	kan^3 chi^1
gray	灰色		whay^1 ser^4	hui^1 sê^4
grease	油泥		yew^2 nee^2	yü^2 ni^2
great	大		dah^4	ta^4
greedy	貪		tahn^1	t'an^1
green	綠色		loo^4 ser^4	lu^4 sê^4

	Chinese	Approximation	Wade
grievance	訴寃	soo⁴ yew-en¹	su⁴ yüan¹
grievous	難受	nahn² shoh¹	nan² shou¹
grocery	雜貨店	dsah² hwor⁴ de-en⁴	tsa² huo⁴ tien⁴
groom	馬夫	mah³ foo¹	ma³ fu¹
ground	地	dee⁴	ti⁴
group	羣種類	chew-n²; joong³ lay⁴	ch'ün²; chung³ lei⁴
grow	生長	shung¹ jong³	shêng¹ chang³
guarantee	担保	dahn¹ baow³	tan¹ pao³
guarantor	保人	baow³ run²	pao³ jên²
guard (n)	衛兵	way⁴ bing¹	wei⁴ ping¹
guard (v)	保護	baow³ hoo⁴	pao³ hu⁴
guess	猜	tsy²	ts'ai²
guest	客人	cur⁴ run²	k'o⁴ jên²
guidance	指導	jir³ daow⁴	chih³ tao⁴
guide (n)	領道的	ling³ daow⁴ dee¹	ling³ tao⁴ ti¹
guide-book	指南	jir³ nahn²	chih³ nan²
guilty	有罪	yoo³ dsoo-ee⁴	yu³ tsui⁴
gunner	礮手	paow⁴ shoh³	p'ao⁴ shou³
gunpowder	火藥	hwor³ yaow	huo³ yao⁴
gunnery	砲術	paow⁴ shoo⁴	p'ao⁴ shu⁴

	Chinese	Approximation	Wade
H			
habit	習慣	she² gwon⁴	hsi² kuan⁴
hair	毛	maow¹	mao²
hair (of head)	髮	fah³	fa³
half	一半	ee' bahn⁴	i' pan⁴
hall	堂廳	tong² ting²	t'ang² t'ing²
halt	停住	ting² joo⁴	t'ing² chu⁴
ham	火腿	hwor³ too-ee³	huo³ t'ui³
hammer (n)	錘子	chway² tze³	ch'ui² tzŭ³
hammer (v)	敲打	che-aow' dah³	ch'iao' ta³
hand	手	shoh³	shou³
handkerchief	手巾	shoh³ jin'	shou³ chin'
handle	把柄	bah⁴ bing³	pa⁴ ping³
handsome	漂亮	pe-aow³ le-ong⁴	p'iao³ liang⁴
handwriting	筆法	bee³ fah³	pi³ fa³
hang	吊掛	de-aow² gwah⁴	tiao² kua⁴
happen	逢巧	fung² che-aow³	fêng² ch'iao³
happiness	幸福	shing⁴ foo²	hsing⁴ fu²
happy	快樂	kwy⁴ law⁴	k'uai⁴ lo⁴
harbor	港口	je-ong³ koh³	chiang³ k'ou³
hard	硬	ying⁴	ying⁴

	Chinese	Approximation	Wade
hard (difficult)	難	nahn^2	nan^2
harm	害	hy^4	hai^4
harmful	有害	yoo^3 hy^4	yu^3 hai^4
harmonious	配合	pay^4 haw^2	p'ei^4 ho^2
harmony	調和	te-aow^2 haw^2	t'iao^2 ho^2
harvest	收成	shoh' chung^2	shou' ch'êng^2
hasten	趕催	gahn; dsway^3	kan; tsui^3
hasty	急忙	jee^2 mong^2	chi^2 mang^2
hat	帽子	maow^4 tze^3	mao^4 tzŭ^3
hate	恨	hun^4	hên^4
hatred	怨恨	yew-en^4 hun^4	yüan^4 hên^4
haul	牽拉	che-en; lah'	ch'ien; la'
have	有	yoo^3	yu^3
hay	乾草	gahn' tsaow^3	kan' ts'ao^3
he	他伊	tah; ee'	t'a; i'
head	頭	toh^2	t'ou^2
headache	頭痛	toh^2 tung^2	t'ou^2 t'êng^2
heal	醫治	ee' jir^4	i' chih^4
healthy	健康	je-en^4 kong'	chien^4 k'ang'
hear	聽聞	ting; wun^2	t'ing; wên^2
heart	心	shin'	hsin'

86

	Chinese	Approximation	Wade
heartbroken	傷心	shong^1 shin^1	shang^1 hsin^1
heat	熱暑	raw^4; shoo^3	jo^4; shu^3
heaven	天堂	te-en^2 tong^2	t'ien^2 t'ang^2
heavy	重	joong^4	chung^4
hell	地獄	dee^{4}yeu^4	ti^4 yü^4
help (n)	幫助	bong^1 joo^4	pang^1 chu^4
help (v)	救	jee-oo^4	chiu
hemp	麻	mah^2	ma^2
hen	母鷄	moo^3 jee^1	mu^3 chi^1
her	她	tah^1	t'a^1
herd	一羣	ee^1 chew-n^2	i^1 ch'ün^2
here	這裡	jair^{4}lee^3	chê^4 li^3
hereafter	將来	je-ong^1 ly^2	chi'ang^1 lai^2
hers (or his)	他的	tah^1 dee^1	t'a^1 ti^1
hero	英雄	ying^1 she-oong^2	ying^1 hsiung^2
hide (n)	皮革	pee^1 gur^2	p'i^1 ko^2
hide (v)	藏	tsong^2	ts'ang^2
high	高	gaow^1	kao^1
highway	公路	goong^1 loo^1	kung^1 lu^4
him	他	tah^1	t'a^1
hinder	阻碍	dsoo^3 ai^1	tsu^3 ai^1

	Chinese	Approximation	Wade
hire	雇	goo⁴	ku⁴
his (or hers)	他的	tah¹dee¹	t'a¹ti¹
history	歷史	lee⁴shir³	li⁴shih³
hit	打中	dah³joong⁴	ta³chung⁴
hoe (n)	鋤子	choo²tze³	ch'u²tzŭ³
hoe (v)	鋤地	choo²dee⁴	ch'u²ti⁴
hog	猪	joo¹	chu¹
hold	拿住	nah²joo⁴	na²chu⁴
hold responsible	負責	foo⁴dseh²	fu⁴tsê²
hole	洞	doong⁴	tung⁴
holiday	假期	jar²chee²	chia²ch'i²
holy	聖的	shung⁴dee¹	shêng⁴ti¹
home	家	jar¹	chia¹
homesickness	想家	she-ong³jar¹	hsiang³chia¹
honest	誠實	chung²shir²	ch'êng²shih²
honesty	誠實	chung²shir²	ch'êng²shih²
honorable	尊貴	dsoo-n¹gway⁴	tsun¹kuei⁴
hope	希望	she¹wong⁴	hsi¹wang⁴
horizontal	橫的	hung⁴dee¹	hêng⁴ti¹
horn	角	je-aow³	chiao³
horse	馬	mah³	ma³

	Chinese	Approximation	Wade
hospitable	好客	haow^3 cur^4	hao^3 k'o^4
hospital	醫院	ee' yew-en^4	i' yüan^4
host	主人	joo^3 run^2	chu jên^2
hostess	女主人	neu^3 joo^3 run^2	nü^3 chu jên^2
hot	熱	raw^4	jo^4
hotel	旅館	leu^3 gwan^3	lü^3 kuan^3
hour	鐘點	joong' de-en^3	chung' tien^3
house	房屋	fong^2 woo'	fang^2 wu'
how	怎樣	dsen^3 yong^4	tsên^3 yang^4
how many	幾個	jee^3 gur^4	chi^3 ko^4
how much	多少	daw' shaow^3	to' shao^3
however	然而	rahn^2 er^2	jan^2 êrh^2
human being	人類	run^2 lay^4	jên^2 lei^4
humble	謙恭	che-en' goong^4	ch'ien' kung^4
hundred	一百	ee' by^3	i' pai^3
hungry	飢餓	jee aw^2	chi' ê^2
hunt	打獵	dah^3 le-eh^4	ta^3 lieh^4
hurry	忙催	mong^2; tsoo-ee'	mang^2; ts'ui'
hurt (verb trans.)	傷	shong'	shang'
hurt (verb intrans.)	受傷	shoh^4 shong'	shou^4 shang'
husband	丈夫	jong^4 foo'	chang^4 fu'

	Chinese	Approximation	Wade
hymn	聖歌	shung⁴ gur¹	shêng⁴ ko¹
I			
I	我	woh³	wo³
ice	冰	bing¹	ping¹
idea	意思	ee⁴ sze¹	i⁴ ssŭ¹
identical	相同	she-ong¹ toong²	hsiang¹ tung²
identify	指出來	jir³ choo¹ ly²	chih³ ch'u¹ lai¹
idle	懶惰	lahn³ daw⁴	lan³ to⁴
if	若	raw⁴	jo⁴
ignorant	無知	woo² jir¹	wu² chih¹
ill	有病	yoo³ bing⁴	yu³ ping⁴
illegal	違法	way¹ fah⁴	wei¹ fa⁴
image	偶像	oh³ she-ong⁴	ou³ hsiang⁴
imagine	設想	sheh⁴ she-ong³	shê⁴ hsiang³
imaginary	空想	koong¹ she-ong³	k'ung¹ hsiang³
imbue	沾,浸	jahn; chin⁴	chan; ch'in⁴
imitate	效法	she-aow² fah³	hsiao² fa³
immediate	立刻	lee⁴ cur⁴	li⁴ k'o⁴
immediately	即刻	jee² cur⁴	chi² k'o⁴
immortal (n)	仙人	shen¹ run²	hsien¹ jên²
immortal (adj)	不朽	boo¹ she-oo³	pu¹ hsiu³

	Chinese	Approximation	Wade
immortality	長生	chong² shung¹	ch'ang² shêng¹
impartial	公平	goong¹ ping²	kung¹ p'ing²
impatient	不耐煩	boo¹ ny⁴ fahn²	pu¹ nai⁴ fan²
impeach	參彈劾	tsahn; tahn² haw²	ts'an; t'an² ho²
implicate	牽連	che-en¹ le-en²	ch'ien¹ lien²
import (n)	輸入品	shoo¹ roo⁴ pin³	shu¹ ju⁴ p'in³
import (v)	進口	jin⁴ koh³	chin⁴ k'ou³
important	緊要	jin³ yaow⁴	chin³ yao⁴
imported	外貨	wy⁴ hwor⁴	wai⁴ huo⁴
importer	進貨的	jin⁴ hwor⁴ dee¹	chin⁴ huo⁴ ti¹
impossible	不可能	boo¹ cur³ nung²	pu¹ k'o³ nêng²
impoverished	貧乏	pin² fah²	p'in² fa²
improper	不正當	boo¹ jung⁴ dong¹	pu¹ chêng⁴ tang¹
improve	改良	guy³ le-ong²	kai³ liang²
in	於在	yeu; dsy⁴	yü; tsai⁴
inch	寸	tsoo-n⁴	ts'un⁴
inclination	偏向	pe-en¹ she-ong⁴	p'ien¹ hsiang⁴
include	包括	baow¹ gwor⁴	pao¹ kua⁴
income	進款	jin⁴ kwon³	chin⁴ k'uan³
incomplete	不完全	boo¹ wan² chew-en²	pu¹ wan² ch'üan²
inconvenient	不便	boo¹ be-en⁴	pu¹ pien⁴

	Chinese	Approximation	Wade
incorrect	不對	boo' doo-ee⁴	pu' tui⁴
increase	加上	jar' shong⁴	chia' shang⁴
indecent	非禮	fay' lee³	fei' li³
indeed	的確	dee' che-aw⁴	ti' ch'io⁴
independence	獨立 自立	doo' lee⁴; tze⁴lee⁴	tu' li⁴; tzǔ⁴ li⁴
India	印度	yin⁴doo⁴	yin⁴ tu⁴
Indian (n)	印度人	yin⁴doo⁴run²	yin⁴ tu⁴jên²
Indian (adj)	印度的	yin⁴doo⁴dee'	yin⁴ tu⁴ti'
indict	控告	koong⁴gaow⁴	k'ung⁴kao⁴
indigestion	胃弱	way⁴raw⁴	wei⁴jo⁴
indigo	藍靛	lahn²de-en⁴	lan²tien⁴
indolent	懶惰	lahn³daw⁴	lan³to⁴
indorse	贊成	dsahn⁴chung²	tsan⁴ch'êng²
indorsement	証明	jung⁴ming²	chêng⁴ming²
induce	使	shir³	shih³
industrial	工藝的	koong'ee⁴dee'	kung'i⁴ti'
industry	實業	shir²yair⁴	shih²yeh⁴
industrious	努力	noo²lee⁴	nu²li⁴
infantry	步兵	boo⁴bing'	pu⁴ping'
infect	傳染	chwon²rahn³	ch'uan²jan³
infectious	傳染的	chwon²rahn³dee'	ch'uan²jan³ti'

	Chinese	Approximation	Wade
inferior	次等	tze⁴dung³	tz'ŭ⁴têng³
infinite	無窮	woo²che-oong²	wu²ch'iung²
inflammation	紅腫	hoong²joong³	hung²chung³
influence	影響	ying³she-ong³	ying³hsiang³
inform	報告	baow⁴gaow⁴	pao⁴kao⁴
information	新聞	shin¹wun²	hsin¹wên²
ingenious	靈巧	ling²che-aow³	ling²ch'iao³
inhabitant	居民	jeu¹min²	chü¹min²
inherit	承繼	chung²jee⁴	ch'êng²chi⁴
iniquity	罪惡	dsway⁴aw⁴	tsui⁴o⁴
initiate	發起	fah¹chee³	fa¹ch'i³
injure	損壞	soo-n³why⁴	sun³huai⁴
injurious	有害的	yoo³hy⁴dee¹	yu³hai⁴ti¹
injustice	不公道	boo¹goong¹daow⁴	pu¹kung¹tao⁴
ink	墨水	maw⁴shway³	mo⁴shui³
inkstand	墨盒	maw⁴haw²	mo⁴ho²
inland	內地	nay⁴dee⁴	nei⁴ti⁴
inn	客店	cur⁴de-en⁴	k'o⁴tien⁴
innocent	無罪	woo²dsway⁴	wu²tsui⁴
insane	痴,發狂	chir¹; fah¹kwong²	ch'ih¹; fa¹k'uang²
insanity	神經病	shun²jing¹bing⁴	shên²ching¹ping⁴

	Chinese	Approximation	Wade
insects	蟲子	choong^2 tze^3	ch'ung^1 tzŭ^3
inside	裏面	lee^3 me-en^4	li^3 mien^4
insight	見地	je-en^4 dee^4	chien^4 ti^4
insignificant	不足輕重	boo^1 dsoo^2 ching^1 joong^4	pu^1 tsu^2 ch'ing^1 chung^4
inspect	檢查	je-en^3 chah^2	chien^3 ch'a^2
inspection	監察	je-en^1 chah^2	chien^1 ch'a^2
instead	代替	dy^4 tee^4	tai^4 t'i^4
instruct	教導	je-aow^4 daow^3	chiao^4 tao^3
instruction	教訓	je-aow^4 shew-n^4	chiao^4 hsün^4
insult	侮辱	woo^2 roo^4	wu^3 ju^4
insurance	保險	baow^3 she-en^3	pao^3 hsien^3
insurrection	暴動	baow^4 doong^4	pao^4 tung^4
intact	完全	wan^2 chew-en^2	wan^2 ch'üan^2
intention	意思	ee^4 sze^1	i^4 ssŭ^1
intentional	故意的	goo^4 ee^4 dee^1	ku^4 i^4 ti^1
intercourse	來往	ly^2 wong^3	lai^2 wang^3
interesting	有趣	yoo^3 cheu^4	yu^3 ch'ü^4
interfere	干預	gahn^1 yeu^4	kan^1 yü^4
interior	裏面	lee^3 me-en^4	li^3 mien^4
international	國際的	gwor^2 jee^4 dee^1	kuo^2 chi^4 ti^1
interpret	繙譯	fahn^1 ee^4	fan^1 i^4

	Chinese	Approximation	Wade
interrupt	中止	joong¹ jir³	chung¹ chih³
interruption	間斷	je-en⁴ dwon⁴	chien⁴ tuan⁴
interval	休息	she-oo¹ she²	hsiu¹ hsi²
interview (n)	會談	whay⁴ tahn²	hui⁴ t'an²
interview (v)	會面	whay⁴ me-en⁴	hui⁴ mien⁴
intimate	親密	chin¹ mee⁴	ch'in¹ mi⁴
introduce	介紹	jair⁴ shaow⁴	chieh⁴ shao⁴
invent	發明	fah¹ ming²	fa¹ ming²
invention	新發明	shin¹ fah¹ ming²	hsin¹ fa¹ ming²
investigate	調查	de-aow⁴ chah²	tiao⁴ ch'a²
investigation	視察	shir⁴ chah²	shih⁴ ch'a²
invitation	請帖	ching³ te-air³	ch'ing³ t'ieh³
invite	請	ching³	ch'ing³
invoice	貨單	hwor⁴ dahn¹	huo⁴ tan¹
inward	向內	she-ong⁴ nay⁴	hsiang⁴ nei⁴
iron	鐵	te-air³	t'ieh³
irritable	容易生氣	roong² ee⁴ shung¹ chee⁴	jung² i⁴ shêng¹ ch'i⁴
is	是	shir⁴	shih⁴
island	島	daow³	tao³
it	其他	chee; tah¹	ch'i²; t'a¹
Italy	義大利	ee⁴ dah⁴ lee⁴	i⁴ ta⁴ li⁴

	Chinese	Approximation	Wade
Italian (n)	義國人	ee⁴ gwor² run²	i⁴ kuo² jên²
Italian (adj)	義國的	ee⁴ gwor² dee¹	i⁴ kuo² ti¹
item	欵目	kwon³ moo⁴	k'uan³ mu⁴
J			
jam	糖醬	tong² je-ong⁴	t'ang² chiang⁴
January	一月	ee¹ yew-eh⁴	i¹ yüeh⁴
Japan	日本	rih⁴ bun³	jih⁴ pên³
Japanese (n)	日本人	rih⁴ bun³ run²	jih⁴ pên³ jên²
Japanese (adj)	日本的	rih⁴ bun³ dee¹	jih⁴ pên³ ti¹
jar	缸	gong¹	kang¹
jest	笑話	she-aow⁴ whah⁴	hsiao⁴ hua⁴
Jew	猶太人	yew² ty⁴ run²	yü² t'ai⁴ jên²
jewel	珍寶	jun¹ baow³	chên¹ pao³
job	工作	goong¹ dsaw⁴	kung¹ tso⁴
join	接合	jair¹ hwor³	chieh¹ huo³
joke (n)	笑話	she-aow⁴ whah⁴	hsiao⁴ hua⁴
joke (v)	説笑話	shoo-aw¹ she-aow⁴ whah⁴	shuo¹ hsiao⁴ hua⁴
journey (n)	路程	loo⁴ chung²	lu⁴ ch'êng²
journey (v)	旅行	leu³ shing²	lü³ hsing²
joy	喜樂	she³ law⁴	hsi³ lo⁴
judge (n)	法官	fah³ gwon¹	fa³ kuan¹

	Chinese	Approximation	Wade
judge (v)	評判	ping² pahn⁴	p'ing² p'an⁴
judgment	判決	pahn⁴ jew-eh²	p'an⁴ chüeh²
jug	瓶,罐	ping²; gwon²	p'ing²; kuan²
juice	汁	jir¹	chih¹
July	七月	chee¹ yew-eh⁴	ch'i¹ yüeh⁴
jump	跳	te-aow⁴	t'iao⁴
June	六月	lee-oo⁴ yew-eh⁴	liu⁴ yüeh⁴
jungle	森林	sun² lin²	sen² lin²
jurisdiction	司法權	sze¹ fah⁴ chew-on²	ssŭ¹ fa⁴ ch'üan²
just	公正	goong¹ jung⁴	kung¹ chêng⁴
justice	正義	jung⁴ ee⁴	chêng⁴ i⁴

K

	Chinese	Approximation	Wade
keep	留,存	lee-oo²; tsoo-n²	liu²; ts'un²
key	鑰匙	yaow⁴ shir³	yao⁴ shih³
kick	踢	tee¹	t'i¹
kill	殺	shah¹	sha¹
kind (sort)	樣子,種類	yong⁴ tze³; joong³ lay⁴	yang⁴ tzŭ³; chung³ lei⁴
kind-hearted	好心	haow³ shin¹	hao³ hsin¹
kindness	仁愛	run² ai¹	jên² ai¹
king	王	wong²	wang²
kingdom	國	gwor²	kuo²

	Chinese	Approximation	Wade
kinship	親戚	chin' chee⁴	ch'in' ch'i⁴
kiss	親嘴	chin' dsway³	ch'in' tsui³
kitchen	厨房	choo² fong²	ch'u² fang²
kitten	小貓	she-aow³ maow'	hsiao³ mao'
knee	膝	she'	hsi'
kneel	跪	gway⁴	kuei⁴
knife	刀	daow'	tao'
knock	敲碰	che-aow'; pung⁴	ch'iao'; p'êng⁴
know	知道	jir' daow⁴	chih' tao⁴
knowledge	知識	jir' shir⁴	chih' shih⁴

L

	Chinese	Approximation	Wade
label	標號	be-aow' haow'	piao' hao'
labor (n)	工役	goong' ee⁴	kung' i⁴
labor (v)	做工	dsaw⁴ goong'	tso⁴ kung'
laborer	工人	goong' run²	kung' jên²
lace	花邊	whah' be-en'	hua' pien'
lack	缺短	chew-eh' dwon³	ch'üeh' tuan³
lad	童子	toong³ tze³	t'ung³ tzŭ³
lady	太太	ty⁴ ty⁴	t'ai⁴ t'ai⁴
lake	湖	hoo⁴	hu⁴
lamb	羊	yong³	yang³

	Chinese	Approximation	Wade
lame	瘸子	chew-eh^2 tze^3	ch'üeh^2 tzŭ^3
lamp	燈	dung^1	têng^1
land (n)	土地,陸地	too^3 dee; loo^4 dee^4	t'u^3 ti; lu^4 ti^4
land (v)	上岸	shong^4 ahn^4	shang^4 an^4
language	語言	yeu^3 yen^2	yü^3 yen^2
lard	猪油	joo^1 yew^2	chu^1 yü^2
large	大	dah^4	ta^4
last	最後	dsway^4 hoh^4	tsui^4 hou^4
late	晚	wan^3	wan^3
laugh	笑	she-aow^4	hsiao^4
laughter	笑聲	she-aow^4 shung^1	hsiao^4 shêng^1
lavatory	便所	be-en^4 saw^3	pien^4 so^3
law	法律	fah^4 leu^4	fa^4 lü^4
lawn	草地	tsaow^3 dee^4	ts'ao^3 ti^4
lawyer	律師	leu^4 shir^1	lü^4 shih^1
lazy	懶惰	lahn^3 daw^4	lan^3 to^4
lead (metal)	鉛	chen^1	ch'ien^1
lead (v)	引導	yin^3 daow^4	yin^3 tao^4
leaf	樹葉	shoo^4 yair^4	shu^4 yeh^4
leak	漏	loh^4	lou^4
lean	靠	kaow^4	k'ao^4

	Chinese	Approximation	Wade
leap	跳	te-aow⁴	t'iao⁴
learn	學習	shoo-er²; she²	hsüeh²; hsi²
lease (n)	祖契	dsoo¹ chee⁴	tsu¹ ch'i⁴
lease (v)	出租	choo¹ dsoo¹	ch'u¹ tsu¹
leave (n)	允許	yew-n³ sheu³	yün³ hsü³
leave (v)	離開	lee² ky¹	li² k'ai¹
lecture	講演	je-ong³ yen³	chiang³ yen³
left (hand)	左	dsaw³	tso³
leg	腿	too-ee³	t'ui³
leisure	閒空	she-en² koong⁴	hsien² k'ung⁴
lemon	檸檬	ning² mung⁴	ning² mêng⁴
lend	借	jair⁴	ohieh⁴
length	長短	chong² dwon³	ch'ang² tuan³
less	少	shaow³	shao³
lesson	功課	goong¹ cur⁴	kung¹ k'o⁴
letter (of alphabet)	字母	tze⁴ moo³	tzŭ⁴ mu³
letter	信	shin⁴	hsin⁴
letter-box	信箱	shin⁴ she-ong⁴	hsin⁴ hsiang⁴
lettuce	生菜	shung¹ tsy⁴	shêng¹ ts'ai⁴
level	平面	ping² me-en⁴	p'ing² mien⁴
levy	徵收	jung¹ shoh¹	chêng¹ shou¹

	Chinese	Approximation	Wade
liar	撒謊的	sah¹ whong³ dee¹	sa¹ huang³ ti¹
liberal	寬大	kwon¹ dah⁴	k'uan¹ ta⁴
library	圖書館	too² shoo² gwon³	t'u² shu² kuan³
lie (n) untruth	謊話	whong³ whah⁴	huang³ hua⁴
lie (v) down	躺下	tong³ shah⁴	t'ang³ hsia⁴
lie (v)	撒謊	sah¹ whong³	sa¹ huang³
life	生命	shung¹ ming⁴	shêng¹ ming⁴
lift	舉起	jeu³ choe³	chü³ ch'i³
light (adj)	輕	ching¹	ch'ing¹
light (n)	陽光	yong² gwong¹	yang² kuang¹
light (v)	點火	de-en³ hwor³	tien³ huo³
light (in color)	淺	che-en³	ch'ien³
lighthouse	燈塔	dung¹ tah³	têng¹ t'a³
lightning	打閃	dah³ shahn³	ta³ shan³
like (adj)	若,如,像	raw⁴; roo²; she-ong⁴	jo⁴; ju²; hsiang⁴
like (v)	喜歡	she³ whon¹	hsi³ huan¹
limb	肢	jir¹	chih¹
limit (n)	限,界	she-en⁴; jair⁴	hsien⁴; chieh⁴
limit (v)	限制	she-en⁴ jir⁴	hsien⁴ chih⁴
limitless	無限	woo² she-en⁴	wu² hsien⁴
line	線行	she-en⁴; hong²	hsien⁴; hang²

|---|---|---|---|
linen	麻布	mah² boo⁴	ma² pu⁴
lining	裏子	lee³ tze³	li³ tzŭ³
lion	獅子	shir¹ tze³	shih¹ tzŭ³
lip	唇	choo-n²	ch'un²
liquor	酒	jee-oo³	chiu³
list	表冊	be-aow³ tseh⁴	piao³ ts'ê⁴
listen	聽	ting¹	ting¹
literate	識字	shir² tze⁴	shih² tzu⁴
literature	文學	wun² shoo-er²	wên² hsüeh²
live	活的	hwor² dee¹	huo² ti¹
live (reside)	住	joo⁴	chu⁴
livelihood	生活	shung¹ hwor²	shêng¹ huo²
lively	活潑	hwor² paw²	huo² p'o²
living	活的	hwor² dee¹	huo² ti¹
load (n)	擔	dahn⁴	tan⁴
load (v)	裝	jwong¹	chuang¹
local	本地	bun³ dee⁴	pên³ ti⁴
lock (n)	鎖	saw³	so³
lock (v)	鎖起來	saw³ chee³ ly²	so³ ch'i³ lai²
lofty	高大	gaow¹ dah⁴	kao¹ ta⁴
London	倫敦	loo-n² doo-n¹	lun² tun¹

	Chinese	Approximation	Wade
long	長	chong^2	ch'ang^2
look	看	kahn^4	k'an^4
look for	找	jaow^3	chao^3
loose	鬆	soong^1	sung^1
lose	輸 失去	shoo^1; shir^1 cheu^3	shu^1; shih^1 ch'ü^3
loss	損失	soo-n^3 shir^1	sun^3 shih^1
love (n)	愛情	ai^4 ching^2	ai^4 ch'ing^2
love (v)	愛	ai^4	ai^4
low	底下	dee; shah^4	ti; hsia^4
loyal	忠心	joong^1 shin^1	chung^1 hsin^1
luck	倖運	shing^4 yew-n^4	hsing^4 yun^4
lucky	交好運	je-aow^1 haow^3 yew-n	chiao^1 hao^3 yün^4
luggage	行李	shing^2 lee^3	hsing^2 li^3
lumber	木料	moo^4 le-aow^4	mu^4 liao^4
lump	塊	kwy^4	k'uai^4
lung	肺	fay^4	fei^4
lust	慾	yeu^4	yü^4
luxuriant	茂盛	maow^4 shung^4	mao^4 shêng^4
M			
machine-gun	機關槍	jee^1 gwon^1 che-ong^1	chi^1 kuan^1 ch'iang^1
machine	機器	jee^1 chee^4	chi^1 ch'i^4

	Chinese	Approximation	Wade
mad	瘋狂	fung; kwong²	fêng; k'uang²
magic	妖術	yaow' shoo⁴	yao' shu⁴
magician	魔術家	maw² shoo⁴ jar'	mo² shu⁴ chia'
magistrate	縣長	she-en⁴ jong²	hsien⁴ chang²
mail (n)	郵件	yoo' je-en⁴	yu² chien⁴
mail (v)	寄	jee⁴	chi⁴
mail box	信箱	shin⁴ she-ong⁴	hsin⁴ hsiang⁴
maintain	維持	way² chir²	wei² ch'ih²
majestic	威嚴	way' yen'	wei' yen'
majesty	尊嚴	dsoo-n' yen'	tsun' yen'
majority	多半	daw' bahn⁴	to' pan⁴
make	為作	way²; dsaw⁴	wei²; tso⁴
male	公雄	goong'; she-oong²	kung'; hsiung²
male principle	陽	yahng²	yang²
malice	惡意	aw⁴ ee⁴	o⁴ i⁴
mama	媽媽	mah' mah'	ma' ma'
man	男人	nahn² run²	nan² jên²
manage	辦理	bahn⁴ lee³	pan⁴ li³
manager	管理人	gwon³ lee³ run²	kuan³ li³ jên²
Mandarin	官	gwon'	kuan'
Mandarin dialect	官話	gwon' whah⁴	kuan' hua⁴

104

	Chinese	Approximation	Wade
manifest (adj)	顯明	she-en³ ming²	hsien³ ming²
manifest (v)	表示	be-aow³ shir⁴	piao³ shih⁴
manly	丈夫氣	jong⁴ foo' chee⁴	chang⁴ fu' ch'i⁴
manner	神氣	shun² chee⁴	shên² ch'i⁴
manners	禮貌	lee³ maow⁴	li³ mao⁴
manufacture	製造	jir⁴ dsaow⁴	chih⁴ tsao⁴
manufacturer	製造家	jir⁴ dsaow⁴ jar'	chih⁴ tsao⁴ chia'
many	多	daw'	to'
map (n)	地圖	dee⁴ too²	ti⁴ t'u²
map (v)	計劃	jee⁴ whah⁴	chi⁴ hua⁴
March	三月	sahn' yew-eh⁴	san' yüeh⁴
march (v)	步行	boo⁴ shing²	pu⁴ hsing²
market	菜市	tsy⁴ shir⁴	ts'ai⁴ shih⁴
marriage	婚姻	hoo-n' yin'	hun' yin'
marriage go-between	媒人	may² run²	mei² jên²
marry (a husband)	嫁	jar⁴	chia⁴
marry (a wife)	娶	cheu³	ch'ü³
master	主人	joo³ run²	chu³ jên²
mat	蓆子	she² tze³	hsi² tzŭ³
match (v)	配合	pay⁴ haw²	p'ei⁴ ho²
matches	洋火	yong² hwor³	yang² huo³

	Chinese	Approximation	Wade
mate	配偶	pay⁴ oh³	p'ei⁴ ou³
material	材料	dsy² le-aow⁴	tsai¹ liao⁴
mathematics	數學	shoo⁴ shoo-er²	shu⁴ hsüeh¹
matter	物質	woo² jir³	wu² chih³
mattress	褥子	roo⁴ tze³	ju⁴ tzŭ³
May	五月	woo³ yew-eh⁴	wu³ yüeh⁴
may	可以	cur² ee³	k'o² i³
me	我	woh³	wo³
meadow	草地	tsaow³ dee⁴	ts'ao³ ti⁴
meal	飯	fahn⁴	fan⁴
mean (adj)	下賤	shah⁴ je-en⁴	hsia⁴ chien⁴
mean (v)	意思	ee⁴ szo¹	i⁴ ssŭ¹
measles	出疹子	choo¹ jun³ tze³	ch'u¹ chên³ tzŭ³
measure (n)	尺度	chir³ doo⁴	ch'ih³ tu⁴
measure (v)	測量	tseh⁴ le-ong²	ts'ê⁴ liang²
meat	肉	roh⁴	jou⁴
medicine	藥	yaow⁴	yao⁴
Mediterranean	地中海	dee⁴ joong¹ hy³	ti⁴ chung¹ hai³
meet (v)	迎接	ying² jair¹	ying² chieh¹
meeting	相會	she-ong¹ whay⁴	hsiang¹ hui⁴
melancholy	憂悶	yoo¹ mun⁴	yu¹ mên⁴

	Chinese	Approximation	Wade
melon	瓜	gwah¹	kua¹
melt	消化	she-aow¹ whah⁴	hsiao¹ hua⁴
member	會員	whay⁴ yew-en²	hui⁴ yüan²
memorandum	節略	jair² lew-eh⁴	chieh² lüeh⁴
mend	修理	she-oo¹ lee³	hsiu¹ li³
mention (n)	記載	jee⁴ dsy⁴	chi⁴ tsai⁴
mention (v)	提起	dee² chee³	ti² ch'i³
merchandise	貨物	hwor⁴ woo⁴	huo⁴ wu⁴
merchant	商人	shong¹ run²	shang¹ jên²
merciful	慈悲	tze² bay¹	ts'ü² pei¹
mercy	慈悲心	tze² bay¹ shin¹	ts'ü² pei¹ hsin¹
merely	不過只	boo² gwor⁴; jir³	pu² kuo⁴; chih³
meridian	子午線	tze³ woo³ she-en⁴	tzŭ³ wu³ hsien⁴
merit (n)	功績	goong¹ jee¹	kung¹ chi¹
merit (v)	應得	ying¹ deh²	ying¹ tê²
meritorious	有功	yoo³ goong¹	yu³ kung¹
messenger	聽差	ting¹ chy¹	t'ing¹ ch'ai¹
metal	金類	jin¹ lay⁴	chin¹ lei⁴
metaphysics	形而上學	shing¹ er² shong⁴ shoo-er²	hsing² êrh² shang⁴ hsüeh²
meteor	流星	lee-oo² shing¹	liu² hsing¹
method	方法	fong¹ fah²	fang¹ fa²

	Chinese	Approximation	Wade
methodical	有條理	yoo³ te-aow² lee⁴	yu³ t'iao² li⁴
microscope	顯微鏡	she-en² way¹ jing⁴	hsien² wei¹ ching⁴
mid-day	中午	joong¹ woo³	chung¹ wu³
middle (adj)	中	joong¹	chung¹
middle (n)	中間	joong¹ je-en⁴	chung¹ chien⁴
midnight	半夜	bahn⁴ yair⁴	pan⁴ yeh⁴
mighty	偉大	way³ dah⁴	wei³ ta⁴
mile	英里	ying¹ lee³	ying¹ li³
military	軍事上	jew-n⁴ shir⁴ shong⁴	chün¹ shih⁴ shang⁴
milk	奶	ny³	nai³
millet	粟	shoo³	shu³
million	百萬	by³ wan⁴	pai³ wan⁴
mind	心	shin¹	hsin¹
mine (n)	礦	kwong⁴	k'uang⁴
mine (adj)	我的	woh³ dee¹	wo³ ti¹
minerals	礦物	kwong⁴ woo⁴	k'uang⁴ wu⁴
miner	礦夫	kwong⁴ foo¹	k'uang⁴ fu¹
mint	造幣廠	dsaow⁴ bee⁴ chong³	tsao⁴ pi⁴ ch'ang³
minus	減	je-en³	chien³
minute (n)	分	fun¹	fên¹
minute (adj)	細	she⁴	hsi⁴

	Chinese	Approximation	Wade
miracle	怪事	gwy⁴ shir⁴	kuai⁴ shih⁴
mirror	鏡子	jing⁴ tze³	ching⁴ tzŭ³
miser	財奴	tsy² neu²	ts'ai² nü²
miserable	可憐	cur² le-en²	k'o² lien²
miserly	看錢重	kahn¹ che-en² joong⁴	k'an¹ ch'ien² chung⁴
misfortune	禍	hwor⁴	huo⁴
misinterpret	誤解	woo⁴ jair³	wu⁴ chieh³
miss	姑娘	goo¹ nee-ong²	ku¹ niang²
mission	差使	chy¹ shir³	ch'ai¹ shih³
missionary	教士	je-aow¹ shir⁴	chiao¹ shih⁴
mistake	錯誤	tsaw⁴ woo⁴	ts'o⁴ wu⁴
mix (v)	混合	hoo-n⁴ haw²	hun⁴ ho²
mobile	活動	hwor² doong⁴	huo² tung⁴
moderate (adj)	和平	haw² ping²	ho² p'ing²
moderate	穩健派	wun³ je-en⁴ py⁴	wên³ chien⁴ p'ai⁴
moderation	節度	jair² doo⁴	chieh² tu⁴
moment	片刻	pe-en⁴ cur⁴	p'ien⁴ k'o⁴
monastery	寺院	sze⁴ yew-en⁴	ssŭ⁴ yüan⁴
Monday	星期一	shing¹ chee² ee¹	hsing¹ ch'i² i¹
money	錢	che-en²	ch'ien²
money-order	滙票	whay⁴ pe-aow⁴	hui⁴ p'iao⁴

109

	Chinese	Approximation	Wade
monkey	猴子	hoh² tze³	hou² tzŭ³
month	月	yew-eh⁴	yüeh⁴
moon	月亮	yew-eh⁴ le-ong⁴	yüeh⁴ liang⁴
moonlight	月光	yew-eh⁴ kwong¹	yüeh⁴ kuang¹
moral	良心	le-ong² shin¹	liang² hsin¹
morality	道德	daow⁴ deh²	tao⁴ tê²
more	多	daw¹	to¹
moreover	而且	er¹ chair³	êrh² ch'ieh³
morning	早晨	dsaow³ chun²	tsao³ ch'ên²
mortal (n)	壽終	shoh⁴ joong⁴	shou⁴ chung⁴
mortal (adj)	人間	run² je-en¹	jên² chien¹
mortality	死亡數	sze³ wong² shoo⁴	ssŭ³ wang² shu⁴
Moscow	莫斯科	maw⁴ sze¹ kaw¹	mo⁴ ssŭ¹ k'o¹
mosquito	蚊蟲	wun² choong²	wên² ch'ung²
mother	母親	moo³ chin¹	mu³ ch'in¹
mother-in-law	岳母	yew-eh⁴ moo³	yüeh⁴ mu³
motion	行動	shing²; doong⁴	hsing²; tung⁴
motion pictures	電影	de-en⁴ ying³	tien⁴ ying³
motive	起意	chee³ ee⁴	ch'i³ i⁴
mount	登上	dung; shong⁴	têng; shang⁴
mountain	山	shahn¹	shan¹

	Chinese	Approximation	Wade
mouse	耗子	haow⁴ tze³	hao⁴ tzŭ³
mouth	嘴 口	dsoo-ee³; koh³	tsui³; k'ou³
move (v. tr.)	移動	ee² doong⁴	i² tung⁴
move (v. intr.)	動	doong⁴	tung⁴
Mr.	先生	she-en¹ shung¹	hsien¹ shêng¹
Mrs.	夫人 太太	foo¹ run²; ty⁴ ty⁴	fu¹ jên²; t'ai⁴ t'ai⁴
much	多	daw¹	to¹
mud	泥土	nee² too³	ni² t'u³
mulberry	桑樹	song¹ shoo⁴	sang¹ shu⁴
mule	騾子	law² tze³	lo² tzŭ³
multiply	加倍	jar¹ bay²	chia¹ pei²
muscle	筋肉	jin¹ roh⁴	chin¹ jou⁴
muscular	筋力	jin¹ lee⁴	chin¹ li⁴
mushrooms	蘑菇	maw² goo¹	mo² ku¹
museum	博物院	baw⁴ yoo⁴ yew-en⁴	po⁴ wu⁴ yüan⁴
music	音樂	yin¹ yew-eh⁴	yin¹ yüeh⁴
musician	音樂家	yin¹ yew-eh⁴ jar¹	yin¹ yüeh⁴ chia¹
must	必須	bee⁴ sheu¹	pi⁴ hsü¹
mutton	羊肉	yong² roh⁴	yang² jou⁴
mutual	互相	hoo⁴ she-ong¹	hu⁴ hsiang¹
my	我的	woh³ dee¹	wo³ ti¹

	Chinese	Approximation	Wade
myself	我自己	woh³ tze⁴ jee³	wo³ tzŭ⁴ chi³
myth	神話	shun² whah⁴	shên² hua⁴

N

	Chinese	Approximation	Wade
nail	釘子	ding¹ tze³	ting¹ tzŭ³
name	姓名	shing⁴ ming²	hsing⁴ ming²
Nanking	南京	nahn² jing¹	nan² ching¹
narrow	窄狹	jy³; shah²	chai³; hsia²
nation	國家	gwor² jar¹	kuo² chia¹
natural	自然	tze⁴ rahn²	tzŭ⁴ jan²
nature	天性	te-en¹ shing⁴	t'ien¹ hsing⁴
navy	海軍	hy³ jew-n¹	hai³ chün¹
near	近	jin⁴	chin⁴
nearly	差不多	chah¹ boo⁴ daw¹	ch'a¹ pu⁴ to¹
necessary	必要,不能少	bee⁴ yaow⁴; boo¹ nung² shaow³	pi⁴ yao⁴; pu¹ nêng² shao³
neck	頸	ching³	ch'ing³
need (n)	需要	sheu¹ yaow⁴	hsü¹ yao⁴
need (v)	要	yaow⁴	yao⁴
needle	針	jun¹	chên¹
negotiate	商議	shong¹ ee⁴	shang¹ i⁴
negotiation	交涉	je-aow¹ sheh⁴	chiao¹ shê⁴
negro	黑人	hay¹ run²	hei¹ jên²

English	Chinese	Approximation	Wade
neighbor	鄰居	lin² jeu¹	lin² chü¹
neighborhood	鄰里	lin² lee³	lin² li³
nephew	姪兒,外甥	jir³ er; wy⁴ shung¹	chih³ êrh;² wai⁴ shêng¹
nerve	神經	shun² jing¹	shên² ching¹
new	新	shin¹	hsin¹
news	新聞	shin¹ wun²	hsin¹ wên²
newspaper	報紙	baow⁴ jir³	pao⁴ chih³
New York	紐約	nee-u³ yaw¹	niu³ yo¹
next	次,第二	tze⁴; dee⁴ er⁴	t'zu⁴; ti⁴ êrh⁴
nib	筆尖	bee³ je-en¹	pi³ chien¹
niece	姪女,外甥女	jir² neu; wy⁴ shung¹ neu⁴	chih² nü;⁴ wai⁴ shêng¹ nü⁴
night	夜	yair⁴	yeh⁴
no	不是	boo¹ shir⁴	pu¹ shih⁴
nod	點頭	de-en³ toh²	tien³ t'ou²
noise	聲音	shung¹ yin¹	shêng¹ yin¹
noodles	麵條	me-en⁴ te-aow²	mien⁴ t'iao²
noon	午時	woo³ shir²	wu³ shih²
north	北	bay³	pei³
north-east	東北	doong¹ bay³	tung¹ pei³
north-west	西北	she¹ bay³	hsi¹ pei³
nose	鼻子	bee² tze³	pi² tzŭ³

	Chinese	Approximation	Wade
not	無, 不	woo^2; boo^1	wu^2; pu^1
not yet	未	way^4	wei^4
note (n)	記 載	jee^4 dsy^4	chi^4 tsai^4
note (v)	注 意	joo^4 ee^4	chu^4 i^4
note-book	簿 子	boo^4 tze^3	pu^4 tzŭ^3
note-paper	紙	jir^3	chih^3
nothing	無	woo^2	wu^2
notice	佈 告	boo^4 gaow^4	pu^4 kao^4
noun	名 詞	ming^2 tze^2	ming^2 tzŭ^2
nourish	養, 育	yong^3; yeu^4	yang^3; yü^4
nourishment	滋 養	tze^1 yong^3	tzŭ^1 yang^3
novel (n)	小 說	she-aow^3 shoo-aw^1	hsiao^3 shuo^1
novel (adj)	新	shin^1	hsin^1
November	十一月	shir^2 ee^1 yew-eh^4	shih^2 i^1 yüeh^4
novice	生 手, 學 徒	shung^1 shoh;^{3} shoo-er^2 too^2	shêng^1 shou;^{3} hsüeh^2 t'u^2
now	今 現 在	jin; she-en^4 dsy^4	chin; hsien^4 tsai^4
number	號 數	haow^4 shoo^3	hao^4 shu^3
numerous	繁 多	fahn^2 daw^1	fan^2 to^1
nurse (children's)	奶 媽	ny^3 mah^1	nai^3 ma^1
nurse (hospital)	看 護 婦	kahn^4 hoo^4 foo^4	k'an^4 hu^4 fu^4
nut	核 兒	haw^2 er^2	ho^2 êrh^2

O

		Approximation	Wade
oak	橡樹	she-ong⁴ shoo⁴	hsiang⁴ shu⁴
oar	槳	jeong³	chiang³
oats	麥子	my⁴ dze³	mai⁴ tzŭ³
obedience	服從	foo² tsoong²	fu² ts'ung²
obey	聽命	ting¹ ming⁴	t'ing¹ ming⁴
object (n)	物	woo⁴	wu⁴
object (v)	反對	fahn² doo-ee⁴	fan² tui⁴
obliterate	除去	choo² cheu⁴	chu² ch'ü⁴
observation	觀察	gwan¹ chah²	kuan¹ ch'a²
observe	注意	joo⁴ ee⁴	chu⁴ i⁴
obstinate	頑固	wan² koo⁴	wan² ku⁴
obstruct	阻礙	dsoo³ ai⁴	tsu³ ai⁴
occasion	時會	shir² whay⁴	shih² hui⁴
occupation	職業	jir² yair⁴	chih² yeh⁴
occupy	占領	jahn¹ ling²	chan¹ ling²
ocean	海洋	hy³ yong²	hai³ yang²
October	十月	shir² yew-eh⁴	shih² yüeh⁴
odd	古怪	koo³ gwy⁴	ku³ kuai⁴
of course	自然	tze⁴ rahn²	tsŭ⁴ jan²
offence	罪	dsoo-ee⁴	tsui⁴

	Chinese	Approximation	Wade
offend	得罪	deh² dsoo-ee⁴	t'ê² tsui⁴
offer	供獻	goong¹ she-en⁴	kung¹ hsien⁴
office	辦公室	bahn⁴ goong¹ shir⁴	pan⁴ kung¹ shih⁴
officer	職員	jir² yew-en²	chih² yüan²
official	公務員	goong¹ woo⁴ yew-en²	kung¹ wu⁴ yüan²
often	常常	chong² chong²	ch'ang² ch'ang²
oil	油	yoo²	yu²
ointment	膏藥	gaow¹ yaow⁴	kao¹ yao⁴
old	老	laow³	lao³
old man	老人	laow³ run²	lao³ jên²
omen	預兆	yeu⁴ jaow⁴	yü⁴ chao⁴
omit	遺忘	ee² wong²	i² wang²
omnibus	公共汽車	koong¹ goong⁴ chee⁴ chair¹	kung¹ kung⁴ ch'i⁴ ch'ê¹
once	一囘	ee¹ whay²	i¹ hui²
one	一	ee¹	i¹
onion	洋蔥	yong² tsoong¹	yang² ts'ung¹
only	惟只	way;² jir³	wei;² chih³
opaque	暗	ahn⁴	an⁴
open	開	ky¹	k'ai¹
operate	作事	dsaw⁴ shir⁴	tso⁴ shih⁴
operation	手術	sho³ shoo⁴	shou³ shu⁴

	Chinese	Approximation	Wade
opinion	意見	ee⁴jen⁴	i⁴ chien⁴
opium	鴉片	yah' pe-en⁴	ya' p'ien⁴
oppose	對抗	doo-ee⁴kong⁴	tui⁴k'ang⁴
opposite	對面	doo-ee⁴me-en⁴	tui⁴mien⁴
optician	眼鏡師	yen³jing⁴shir'	yen³ching⁴shih'
optional	隨意	sway²ee⁴	sui²i⁴
orbit	軌道	gway²daow⁴	kuei²tao⁴
orchid	蘭花	lahn²whah'	lan²hua'
order (n)	次序	tze⁴sheu⁴	ts'ü⁴hsü⁴
order (v)	命令	ming⁴ling⁴	ming⁴ling⁴
ordinary	平常	ping²chong²	p'ing²ch'ang²
ore	礦物	kwong⁴woo⁴	kuang⁴wu⁴
organization	組織	dsoo³jir²	tsu³chih²
Orient	東方	doong'fong'	tung'fang'
origin	原始	yew-en²shir³	yüan²shih³
orphan	孤兒	goo'er²	ku'erh²
other	別的	be-air²dee'	pieh²ti'
ought	應當	ying'dong'	ying'tang'
ounce	兩	le-ong³	liang³
our	我們的	woh³men²dee'	wo³mên²ti'
out	外	wy⁴	wai⁴

	Chinese	Approximation	Wade
outline (n)	大綱	dah^{4}gong^1	ta^{4}kang^1
outside	外面	wy^{4}me-en^4	wai^{4}mien^4
outward	向外	she-ong^{4}wy^4	hsiang^{4}wai^4
oven	爐子	loo^{1}tze^3	lu^{2}tzŭ^3
over	在上	dsy^{4}shong^4	tsai^{4}shang^4
overcoat	外套	wy^{4}taow^4	wai^{4}t'ao^4
overflow	溢出	ee^{4}choo^1	i^{4}ch'u^1
ox	牛	nee-u^2	niu^2
P			
pace	步	boo^4	pu^4
Pacific Ocean	太平洋	ty^{4}ping^{2}yong^2	t'ai^{4}ping^{2}yang^2
pack	裝包	chwong^{1}baow^1	chuang^{1}pao^1
package	包	baow^1	pao^1
pail	桶	toong^3	t'ung^3
pain	痛	toong^4	t'ung^4
painful	痛的	toong^{4}dee^1	t'ung^{4}ti^1
painting	畫	whah^4	hua^4
paint (v)	繪畫	whay^{4}whah^4	hui^{4}hua^4
paints	顏料	yen^{2}le-aow^4	yen^{2}liao^4
pair	一對	ee^{1}doo-ee^4	i^{1}tui^4
pale	變色	be-en^{4}ser^4	pien^{4}sə^4

	Chinese	Approximation	Wade
palm	手掌	sho^3 chong^1	shou^3 chang^1
pan	手盆	pun^2	p'ên^2
pants	褲子	koo^4 tze^3	k'u^4 tzŭ^3
paper	紙	jir^3	chih^3
paragraph	節目	jair^2 moo^4	chieh^2 mu^4
parachute	下落傘	shah^4 law^4 sahn^3	hsia^4 lo^4 san^3
parent	父母	foo^4 moo^3	fu^4 mu^3
Paris	巴黎	pah^1 lee^2	pa^1 li^2
park	公園	goong^1 yew-en^2	kung^1 yüan^2
part (n)	一部份	ee^1 boo^4 fun^1	i^1 pu^4 fên^1
part (v)	分散	fun^1 sahn^4	fên^1 san^4
partition	瓜分	gwah^1 fun^1	kua^1 fên^1
partner	合夥	haw^1 hwor^3	ho^2 huo^3
party	黨派	dong^3 py^4	tang^3 p'ai^4
pass by	走過	dsoh^3 gwor^4	tsou^3 kuo^4
passage	道路	daow^4 loo^4	tao^4 lu^4
passenger	旅客	leu^3 cur^4	lü^3 k'o^4
passion	情感	ching^2 gahn^3	ch'ing^2 kan^3
passport	護照	hoo^4 jaow^4	hu^4 chao^4
paste	漿糊	je-ong^3 hoo^2	chiang^3 hu^2
path	小路	she-aow^3 loo^4	hsiao^3 lu^4

	Chinese	Approximation	Wade
patient	忍耐	run³ ny⁴	jên³ nai⁴
patriotic	愛國	ai⁴ gwor²	ai⁴ kuo²
patriotism	愛國心	ai⁴ gwor² shin¹	ai⁴ kuo² hsin¹
pattern	樣式	yong⁴ shir⁴	yang⁴ shih⁴
pause	停歇	ting² she-eh¹	t'ing² hsieh¹
paid	付了	foo⁴ le-aow³	fu⁴ liao³
pay	付	foo⁴	fu⁴
payment	支付	jir¹ foo⁴	chih¹ fu⁴
peace	平安	ping² ahn¹	p'ing² an¹
peaceful	平靜	ping² jing⁴	p'ing² ching⁴
peach	桃子	taow² tze³	t'ao² tzŭ³
peak	山峰	shahn¹ fung¹	shan¹ fêng¹
peanut	花生	whah¹ shung¹	hua¹ shêng¹
pear	梨	lee²	li²
Pearl	珍珠	jen¹ joo¹	chên¹ chu¹
peasant	農夫	noong² foo¹	nung² fu¹
peculiar	特別	ter⁴ be-air²	t'ê⁴ pieh²
peel	削皮	she-aow¹ pee²	hsiao¹ p'i²
pedestrian	行人	shing² run²	hsing² jên²
Peiping	北平	bay³ ping²	pei³ p'ing²
pen	銅筆	gong¹ bee³	kang¹ pi³

120

	Chinese	Approximation	Wade
pencil	鉛筆	che-en¹ bee³	ch'ien¹ pi³
peninsula	半島	bahn⁴ daow³	pan⁴ tao³
penetrate	穿入	chwan¹ roo⁴	ch'uan¹ ju⁴
pen-knife	小刀	she-aow³ daow¹	hsiao³ tao¹
penny	一分	ee¹ fun¹	i¹ fên¹
people	人民	run²min²	jên² min²
pepper	胡椒	hoo² je-aow¹	hu² chiao¹
perception	知覺	jir¹ jew-eh²	chih¹ chüeh²
perfect	完全	wan² chew-en²	wan² ch'üan²
perfectly	十分	shir² fun¹	shih² fên¹
perform	作	dsaw⁴	tso⁴
perfume	香水	she-ong¹ shway³	hsiang¹ shui³
perhaps	或者	hwor⁴ jaw³	huo⁴ chê³
peril	危險	way¹ she-en³	wei¹ hsien³
period	時期	shir² chee²	shih² ch'i²
permanent	永久	yoong³ jee-oo³	yung³ chiu³
permit	許可	sheu³ cur³	hsü³ k'o³
person	人	run²	jên²
perspire	出汗	choo¹ hahn⁴	ch'u¹ han⁴
persuade	勸告	chew-en⁴ gaow⁴	ch'üan⁴ kao⁴
pewter	錫	she²	hsi²

	Chinese	Approximation	Wade
pharmacy	藥房	yaow⁴ fong²	yao⁴ fang²
philosopher	哲學家	jaw² shoo-er² jar¹	chê² hsüeh² chia¹
philosophy	哲學	jaw² shoo-er²	chê² hsüeh²
phonograph	話匣子	whah⁴ shah² tze³	hua⁴ hsia² tzŭ³
phonograph record	話片	whah⁴ pe-en⁴	hua⁴ p'ien⁴
photograph	照相	jaow⁴ pe-en⁴	chao⁴ p'ien⁴
photographer	照相家	jaow⁴ she-ong¹ jar¹	chao⁴ hsiang¹ chia¹
physics	物理	woo⁴ lee³ shoo-er²	wu⁴ li³ hsüeh²
picture	畫片	whah⁴ pe-en⁴	hua⁴ p'ien⁴
piece	塊	kwy⁴	k'uai⁴
pier	碼頭	mah³ toe²	ma³ t'ou²
pig	猪	joo¹	chu¹
pill	丸藥	wahn² yaow⁴	wan² yao⁴
pillow	枕頭	jen³ toe²	chên³ t'ou²
pilot (n)	機司	jee¹ sze¹	chi¹ ssŭ¹
pin	針	jen¹	chên¹
pink	粉紅	fun³ hoong²	fên³ hung²
pit	坑	kung¹	k'êng¹
pity	可惜	cur³ she¹	k'o³ hsi¹
place	地方	dee⁴ fong¹	ti⁴ fang¹
plague	時疫	shir² ee⁴	shih² i⁴

	Chinese	Approximation	Wade
plain	明白	ming² by²	ming² pai²
plan	計畫	jee⁴ whah⁴	chi⁴ hua⁴
planet	行星	shing² shing¹	hsing² hsing¹
plank	木板	moo⁴ bahn³	mu⁴ pan³
plant (n)	植物	jir² woo⁴	chih² wu⁴
plant (v)	種	joong³	chung³
plate	盤子	pahn³ tze³	p'an³ tzŭ³
platform	臺	ty²	t'ai²
play (n)	戲	she⁴	hsi⁴
play (v)	玩	wahn⁴	wan⁴
please	請	ching³	ch'ing³
pleasure	娛樂	yeu² law⁴	yü² lo⁴
plenty	有餘,多	yoo³ yeu²; daw¹	yu³ yü²; to¹
plough	犁	lee²	li²
pocket	口袋	koh³ dy⁴	k'ou³ tai⁴
plum	梅子	may² tze³	mei² tsŭ³
plus	加	jar¹	chia¹
poet	詩人	shir¹ run²	shih¹ jên²
poetry	詩	shir¹	shih¹
point (n)	尖	je-en¹	chien¹
point (v)	指點	jir³ de-en³	chih³ tien³

123

	Chinese	Approximation	Wade
poison	毒	doo²	tu²
pole	木竿	moo⁴ gahn¹	mu⁴ kan¹
police	巡警	shew-n² jing¹	hsün² ching¹
police-station	警察局	jing¹ chah² jew²	ching¹ ch'a² chü²
polite	有禮	yoo³ lee³	yu³ li³
politics	政治	jun⁴ jir⁴	chên⁴ chih⁴
pond	池	chir²	ch'ih²
pontoon	浮橋	foh² che-aow²	fou² ch'iao²
poor (condition)	窮苦	che-oong² koo³	ch'iung² k'u³
poor (quality)	岁質	le-air⁴ jir²	lieh⁴ chih²
pony	小馬	she-aow³ mah³	hsiao³ ma³
population	人口	run² koh³	jên² k'ou³
pork	猪肉	joo¹ roh⁴	chu¹ jou⁴
port	商埠	shong¹ boo⁴	shang¹ pu⁴
porter	看門的	kahn⁴ mun² dee¹	k'an⁴ mên² ti¹
positive	肯定	kun³ ding⁴	kên³ ting⁴
positively	一定	ee¹ ding⁴	i¹ ting⁴
postage stamp	郵票	yoo² pe-aow⁴	yu² p'iao⁴
post-card	郵片	yoo² pe-en⁴	yu² p'ien⁴
post-man	郵差	yoo² chy¹	yu² ch'ai¹
Post Office	郵政局	yoo² jung⁴ jeu²	yu² chêng⁴ chü²

	Chinese	Approximation	Wade
postpone	延期	yen^2 chee^2	yen^2 ch'i^2
pot	鍋	gwor^1	kuo^1
potato	洋山芋	yong^2 shahn^1 yeu^4	yang^2 shan^1 yü^4
pound	磅	pong^2	p'ang^2
pour	流出	lee-oo^2 choo^1	liu^2 ch'u^1
power	能力	nung^2 lee^4	nêng^2 li^4
practice	練習	le-en^4 she^2	lien^4 hsi^2
practicable	可能的	cur^3 nung^2 dee	k'o^3 nêng^2 ti^1
praise (n)	嘉許	jar^1 sheu^3	chia^1 hsü^3
praise (v)	稱讚	chung^1 dsahn^4	ch'êng^1 tsan^4
pray	禱告	daow^3 gaow^4	tao^3 kao^4
precede	前行	che-en^2 shing^2	ch'ien^2 hsing^2
precious	貴重	gway^4 joong^4	kuei^4 chung^4
predecessor	前人	chen^2 run^2	ch'ien^2 jên^2
predict	預言	yeu^4 yen^2	yü^4 yen^2
pregnant	懷胎	why^4 ty^1	huai^4 t'ai^1
prepare	預備	yeu^4 bay^4	yü^4 pei^4
prescription	藥方	yaow^4 fong^1	yao^4 fang^1
present (gift)	禮物	lee^3 woo^4	li^3 wu^4
present (time)	在場	dsy^4 chong^2	tsai^4 ch'ang^2
present (v)	贈送	jung^4 soong^4	tsêng^4 sung^4

	Chinese	Approximation	Wade
presentiment	預覺	yeu⁴ jee-aw²	yü⁴chio²
press	壓	yah¹	ya¹
pretty	好看	haow³ kahn⁴	hao³ k'an⁴
prevent	預防	yeu⁴ fong²	yü⁴fang²
previous	在前的	dsy⁴ chen² dee¹	tsai⁴ ch'ien² ti¹
previously	早先	dsaow³ she-en¹	tsao³ hsien¹
price	定價	ding⁴ jar⁴	ting⁴ chia⁴
priest	教士	je-aow⁴ shir⁴	chiao⁴ shih⁴
primitive	上古	shong⁴ goo³	shang⁴ ku³
print	印刷	yin⁴ shwah¹	yin⁴ shua¹
printer	印刷人	yin⁴ shwah¹ run²	yin⁴ shua¹ jên²
prison	監牢	jen⁴ laow²	chien⁴ lao²
prisoner	犯人	fahn⁴ run²	fan⁴ jên²
private (adj)	私有	sze¹ yoo³	ssŭ¹ yu³
private (rank)	小兵	she-aow³ bing¹	hsiao³ ping¹
privilege	權利	chew-en² lee⁴	ch'üan² li⁴
probable	也許	yair³ sheu³	yeh³ hsü³
problem	問題	wun⁴ tee²	wên⁴ t'i²
proclaim	宣佈	shew-n¹ boo⁴	hsüan¹ pu⁴
produce	產生	chahn³ shung¹	ch'an³ shêng¹
production	生產	shung¹ chahn³	shêng¹ ch'an³

	Chinese	Approximation	Wade
profession	職業	jir² yair⁴	chih² yeh⁴
profit (n)	利息	lee⁴ she²	li⁴ hsi²
profit (v)	得益	deh² ee²	tê² i²
progress (n)	進步	jin⁴ boo⁴	chin⁴ pu⁴
progress (v)	前進	chen² jin⁴	ch'ien² chin⁴
prohibit	禁止	jin⁴ jir³	chin⁴ chih³
project	計劃	jee⁴ whah⁴	chi⁴ hua⁴
prolific	繁盛	fahn² shung⁴	fan² shêng⁴
promise (n)	允許	yew-n³ sheu³	yün³ hsü³
promise (v)	答應	tah' ying'	t'a' ying'
promote	提倡	tee² chong⁴	t'i² ch'ang⁴
prompt	即刻	jee² cur'	chi² k'o'
pronounce	發音	fah' yin'	fa' yin'
proof	証據	jung' jeu⁴	chêng' chü⁴
proper	正當	jung' dong'	chêng' tang'
property	家產	jar' chahn³	chia' ch'an³
prospectus	章程	jahng' chung²	chang' ch'êng²
prosper	興旺	shing' wong⁴	hsing' wang⁴
prosperity	興旺	shing' wong⁴	hsing' wang⁴
prosperous	興旺	shing' wong⁴	hsing' wang⁴
protect	保護	baow³ hoo⁴	pao³ hu⁴

	Chinese	Approximation	Wade
Protestant	耶蘇教徒	yair¹ soo¹ je-aow⁴ too²	yeh¹ su¹ chiao⁴ tu²
Protestantism	耶蘇教	yair¹ soo¹ je-aow⁴	yeh¹ su¹ chiao⁴
prove	証明	jung ming²	chêng¹ ming²
proverb	格言	gur² yen²	ko² yen²
provisions	食料	shir² le-aow⁴	shih² liao⁴
public (n)	民眾	min² joong⁴	min² chung⁴
public (adj)	公開	goong¹ ky¹	kung¹ k'ai¹
publish	出版	choo¹ bahn³	ch'u¹ pan³
pull	拉	lah¹	la¹
pulse	脈	maw⁴	mo⁴
punctual	準時	jun³ shir²	chun³ shih²
punish	罰	fah²	fa²
pupil	學生	shoo-er² shung¹	hsüeh² shêng¹
puppet (show)	木偶	moo⁴ oh³	mu⁴ ou³
puppet (government)	傀儡	kway³ lay³	k'uei³ lei³
purchase	購買	goh⁴ my³	kou⁴ mai³
pure	純潔	shun² jair²	shun² chieh²
purple	紫色	tze³ ser⁴	tsu³ sê⁴
purposely	故意	goo⁴ ee⁴	ku⁴ i⁴
purse	錢袋	che-en² dy⁴	ch'ien² tai⁴
push	推	too-ay¹	t'ui¹

	Chinese	Approximation	Wade
pursue	追	joo-ay^1	chui^1
put	放, 擱	fong^4; gur^1	fang^4; ko^1
putrid	腐爛	foo^3 lahn^4	fu^3 lan^4
puzzle	謎	mee^3	mi^3
Q			
quality	本質	bun^3 jir^2	pên^3 chih^2
quantity	量	le-ong^2	liang^2
quarrel (n)	口角	koh^3 jee-aw^2	k'ou^3 chio^2
quarrel (v)	爭論	jung^1 loo-n^4	chêng^1 lun^4
quarter	四分之一	sze^4 fun^1 jir^1 ee^1	ssŭ^4 fên^1 chih^1 i^1
queer	古怪	goo^3 kwy^4	ku^3 kuai^4
question (n)	問題	wun^4 tee^2	wên^4 t'i^2
question (v)	問	wun^4	wên^4
quick	快	kwy^4	k'uai^4
quickly	快快的	kwy^4 kwy^4 dee^4	k'uai^4 k'uai^4 ti
quiet	靜	jing^4	ching^4
quilt	被	bay^4	pei^4
quite	十分	shir^2 fun^1	shih^2 fên^1
quinine	金鷄納霜	jin^1 jee^1 nah^4 shwong^1	chin^1 chi^1 na^4 shuang^1
quit	不幹	boo^1 gahn^4	pu^1 kan^4
quote	引用	yin^3 yoong^4	yin^3 yung^4

R

English	Chinese	Approximation	Wade
rabbit	兔子	too^4 tze^3	t'u^4 tzŭ^3
race	賽跑	sy^4 paow^3	sai^4 p'ao^3
race horse	跑馬	paow^3 mah^3	p'ao^3 ma^3
radio	無綫電	woo^2 shen^4 de-en^4	wu^2 hsien^4 tien^4
rag	破布	paw^4 boo^4	p'o^4 pu^4
railway	鐵路	te-air^3 loo^4	t'ieh^3 lu^4
rain (n)	雨	yeu^3	yü^3
rain (v)	下雨	shah^4 yeu^3	hsia^4 yü^3
raincoat	雨衣	yeu^3 ee^1	yü^3 i^1
raise	提起	tee^2 chee^3	t'i^2 ch'i^3
rank (n)	班,等	bahn; dung^3	pan; têng^3
rare	希有	she^1 yoo^3	hsi^1 yu^3
rascal	流氓	lee-oo^2 mong^2	liu^2 mang^2
rash	疹斑	jun^2 bahn^1	chên^2 pan^1
rat	鼠	shoo^3	shu^3
rations	限制糧食	shen^4 jir^4 le-ong^2 shir^2	hsien^4 chih^4 liang^2 shih^2
raw	生的	shung^1 dee^1	shêng^1 ti^1
rayon	人造絲	run^2 dsaow^4 sze^1	jên^2 tsao^4 su^1
razor	剃刀	tee^4 daow^1	t'i^4 tao^1
reach	到	daow^4	tao^4

	Chinese	Approximate	Wade
read	念書	ne-en⁴ shoo¹	nien⁴ shu¹
ready	預備	yeu⁴ bay⁴	yü⁴ pei⁴
ready-made	現成	she-en⁴ chung²	hsien⁴ ch'êng²
real	真實	jun; shir¹	chên; shih¹
realize	實現	shir² she-en⁴	shih² hsien⁴
reason	理論	lee³ loo-n⁴	li³ lun⁴
rebel (n)	叛徒	pahn⁴ too²	p'an⁴ t'u²
rebel (v)	造反	dsaow⁴ fahn²	tsao⁴ fan²
rebuke	責備	dseh² bay⁴	tsê̂² pei⁴
receipt	收條	sho¹ te-aow²	shou¹ t'iao²
receive	收到	sho¹ daow⁴	shou¹ tao⁴
receiver	受主	sho⁴ joo³	shou⁴ chu³
recent	新近	shin¹ jin⁴	hsin¹ chin⁴
reception	歡迎會	whon¹ ying² whay⁴	huan¹ ying² hui⁴
recipe	食譜	shir² poo³	shih² p'u³
reciprocal	相互的	she-ong¹ hoo⁴ dee¹	hsiang¹ hu⁴ ti¹
reckon	計算	jee⁴ swon⁴	chi⁴ suan⁴
recognize	認得	run⁴ deh²	jên⁴ tê̂²
recommend	保舉	baow³ jeu³	pao³ chü³
reconcile	調停	te-aow² ting²	t'iao² t'ing²
record	紀錄	jee⁴ loo⁴	chi⁴ lu⁴

	Chinese	Approximation	Wade
record (v)	記載	jee⁴ dsy⁴	chi⁴ tsai⁴
recover	復原	foo⁴ yew-en²	fu⁴ yüan²
red	紅	hoong²	hung²
Red Cross	紅十字會	hoong² shir² tze⁴ whay⁴	hung² shih² tsŭ⁴ hui⁴
reduce	減少	je-en³ shaow³	chien³ shao³
refine	精製	jing¹ jir⁴	ching¹ chih⁴
refined	文雅	wun² yah³	wên² ya³
reflect	反照	fahn² jaow⁴	fan² chao⁴
reform	改良	guy³ le-ong²	kai³ liang²
refuge	避難所	bee⁴ nahn² saw³	pi⁴ nan² so³
refugee	難民	nahn² min²	nan² min²
refuse (v)	拒絕	jeu⁴ jew-eh²	chü⁴ chüeh²
regard	注意	joo⁴ ee⁴	chu⁴ i⁴
region	地方	dee⁴ fong¹	ti⁴ fang¹
register	登記	dung¹ jee⁴	têng¹ chi⁴
registrar	登記員	dung¹ jee⁴ yew-en²	têng¹ chi⁴ yüan²
registration	註冊	joo⁴ tse⁴	chu⁴ tsê⁴
regress	退步	too-ee⁴ boo⁴	t'ui⁴ pu⁴
regret	抱歉	baow⁴ jen⁴	pao⁴ chien⁴
regular	照常	jaow¹ jong²	chao¹ chang²
rejoice	歡喜	whon¹ she³	huan¹ hsi³

	Chinese	Approximation	Wade
relationship	關係	gwan' she⁴	kuan' hsi⁴
relative	親戚	chin' chee⁴	ch'in' ch'i⁴
release	放去	fong' cheu⁴	fang' ch'ü⁴
religion	宗教	dsoong' je-aow⁴	tsung' chiao⁴
religious	宗教的	dsoong' je-aow⁴ dee'	tsung' chiao⁴ ti'
reluctant	不願	boo' yew-en⁴	pu' yüan⁴
rely	靠	kaow⁴	k'ao⁴
remain	留	lee-oo²	liu²
remainder	下存	shah⁴ tsoo-n²	hsia⁴ ts'un²
remark	觀察	gwan' chah²	kuan' ch'a²
remarkable	非常	fay' chong²	fei' ch'ang²
remember	記得	jee⁴ deh²	chi⁴ tê²
remind	提醒	tee' shing³	t'i' hsing³
remote	遠的	yew-en³ dee'	yüan³ ti'
remove	搬去	bahn' cheu³	pan' ch'ü³
render	給	gay³	kei³
rent (n)	租金	dsoo' jin'	tsu' chin'
rent (v)	出租	choo' dsoo'	ch'u' tsu'
repair	修理	shee-oo' lee³	hsiu' li³
repay	報告	baow⁴ dah²	pao⁴ ta²
repent	後悔	hoh⁴ whay³	hou⁴ hui³

	Chinese	Approximation	Wade
reply	回答	whay² dah²	hui² ta²
report	報告	baow⁴ gaow⁴	pao⁴ kao⁴
repose	安靜	ahn¹ jing⁴	an¹ ching⁴
represent	代表	dy⁴ be-aow³	tai⁴ piao³
reprove	責備	dseh² bay⁴	tsê² pei⁴
republic	共和國	gung⁴ haw² gwor²	kung⁴ ho² kuo²
request	請求	ching³ chee-oo²	ch'ing³ ch'iu²
require	需要	sheu¹ yaow⁴	hsü¹ yao⁴
rescue	救	jee-oo⁴	chiu⁴
resemble	相像	she-ong¹ she-ong⁴	hsiang¹ hsiang⁴
reserve	預定	yeu⁴ ding⁴	yü⁴ ting⁴
reserves	預備軍	yeu⁴ bay⁴ jew-n¹	yü⁴ pei⁴ chün¹
reservoir	水池	shway³ chir²	shui³ ch'ih²
residue	剩	shung⁴	shêng⁴
resign	辭職	tse² jir²	ts'ü² chih²
resist	抵抗	dee³ kong⁴	ti³ k'ang⁴
resolution	定志	ding⁴ jir⁴	ting⁴ chih⁴
resolve	決意	jew-eh² ee⁴	chüeh² i⁴
respect	敬重	jing⁴ joong⁴	ching⁴ chung⁴
respond	答應	dah² ying⁴	ta² ying⁴
responsible	負責	foo⁴ dseh²	fu⁴ tsê²

	Chinese	Approximation	Wade
responsibility	責任	dseh² run⁴	tsê² jên⁴
rest	休息	she-oo' she'	hsiu' hsi'
restaurant	飯店	fahn⁴ de-en⁴	fan⁴ tien⁴
restriction	限制	she-en⁴ jir⁴	hsien⁴ chih⁴
result	結果	jair² gwor³	chieh² kuo³
resume	恢復	whay' foo⁴	hui' fu⁴
retail	零售	ling² sho⁴	ling² shou⁴
retire	引退	yin³ too-ay⁴	yin³ t'ui⁴
retreat	退避	too-ay⁴ bee⁴	t'ui⁴ pi⁴
return	歸還 回	gway' whon; whay²	kuei' huan; hui²
revenge	報復	baow⁴ foo⁴	pao⁴ fu⁴
revenue	進款	jin⁴ kwon³	chin⁴ k'uan³
revert	反轉	fahn² jwon³	fan² chuan³
revive	蘇醒	soo' shing³	su' hsing³
revolution	革命	gur² ming⁴	ko² ming⁴
revolver	手槍	sho³ che-ong'	shou³ ch'iang'
reward	酬報	cho² baow⁴	ch'ou² pao⁴
rice	米	mee³	mi³
rice (cooked)	飯	fahn⁴	fan⁴
rice (growing)	稻	daow⁴	tao⁴
rich	富有	foo⁴ yoo³	fu⁴ yu³

	Chinese	Approximation	Wade
ride	乘 坐	chen²; dsaw⁴	ch'en²; tso⁴
ridicule	譏 笑	jee' she-aow⁴	chi' hsiao⁴
ridiculous	可 笑	cur³ she-aow⁴	k'o³ hsiao⁴
rifle	槍	che-ong'	ch'iang'
right (proper)	對	doo-ee⁴	tui⁴
right (hand)	右	yoo⁴	yu⁴
right-angle	直 角	jir² jee-aw²	chih² chio²
righteousness	正 義	jung⁴ ee⁴	chêng⁴ i⁴
right hand	右 手	yoo⁴ sho³	yu⁴ shou³
rights	權 利	chew-an²lee⁴	ch'üan²li⁴
rim	邊	be-en'	pien'
ring	圈	chew-en'	ch'üan'
riot	暴 動	baow⁴doong⁴	pao⁴tung⁴
ripe	熟	shoo²	shu²
rise	漲	jong⁴	chang⁴
rise (in price)	漲 價	jong⁴ jar⁴	chang⁴ chia⁴
risk	冒 險	mao⁴she-en³	mao⁴hsien³
rival	對 敵	doo-ee⁴dee²	tui⁴ti²
river (small)	河	haw²	ho²
river (big)	江	je-ong'	chiang'
road	道 路	daow⁴ loo⁴	tao⁴lu⁴

	Chinese	Approximation	Wade
roar	吼	hoh^3	hou^3
roast	烤	kaow^3	k'ao^3
rob	搶	che-ong^3	ch'iang^3
robber	強盜	che-ong^2 daow^4	ch'iang^2 tao^4
robust	強壯	che-ong^2 jwong^4	ch'iang^2 chuang^4
rock	石頭	shir^2 toe^2	shih^2 t'ou^2
roll	滾	koo-n^3	kun^3
rolling-pin	麵棍	me-en^4 koo-n^4	mien^4 kun^4
Rome	羅馬	law^2 mah^3	lo^2 ma^3
roof	屋頂	woo^1 ding^3	wu^1 ting^3
room	房屋	fong^2 woo^1	fang^2 wu^1
root	根	gun^1	kên^1
rope	繩	shung^3	shêng^3
rose	玫瑰花	may^2 gway^1 whah^1	mei^2 kuei^1 hua^1
rotten	腐爛	foo^3 lahn^4	fu^3 lan^4
rough	粗魯	tsoo^1 loo^3	t'su^1 lu^3
round	圓	yew-en^2	yüan^2
route	行程	shing^2 ching^2	hsing^2 ch'êng^2
row	行列	hong^2 le-air^4	hang^2 lieh^4
rub	摩擦	maw^2 tsah^1	mo^2 ts'a^1
rude	無禮貌	woo^2 lee^3 maow^4	wu^2 li^3 mao^4

	Chinese	Approximation	Wade
rug	地毯	dee' tahn^3	ti' t'an^3
rule (n)	規則	gway' dseh^2	kuei' tsê$\hat{}^2$
rule (v)	治理	jir^4 lee^3	chih^4 li^3
ruler	尺	chir^3	ch'ih^3
rumour	謠言	yaow^2 yen^2	yao^2 yen^2
run	跑	paow^3	p'ao^3
rush	衝	choong'	ch'ung'
Russia	俄國	oh^2 gwor^2	ô^2 kuo^2
Russian (n)	俄國人	oh^2 gwor^2 run^2	ô^2 kuo^2 jên^2
Russian (adj)	俄國的	oh' gwor^2 dee'	ô' kuo^2 ti'
rust	鐵銹	te-air^3 she-oo^4	t'ieh^3 hsiu^4
S			
Sabbath	安息日	ahn' she^2 rih^4	an' hsi^2 jih^4
sack	袋	dy^4	tai^4
sacred	神聖的	shun^2 shung^4 dee'	shên^2 shêng^4 ti'
sad	悲傷	bay' shong'	pei' shang'
safe	平安	ping^2 ahn'	p'ing^2 an'
sage	聖人	shung^4 run^2	shêng^4 jên^2
sail (n)	帆	fahn^2	fan^2
sail (v)	航行	hong^2 shing^2	hang^2 hsing^2
sailor	水手	shway^3 sho^3	shui^3 shou^3

	Chinese	Approximation	Wade
salary	薪水	shin¹ shway³	hsin¹ shui³
sale	出售	choo¹ sho⁴	ch'u¹ shou⁴
salesman	售貨人	sho⁴ hwor⁴ run²	shou⁴ huo⁴ jên²
salt	鹽	yen²	yen²
salute	行禮	shing² lee³	hsing² li³
salvation	救濟	jee-oo⁴ jee⁴	chiu⁴ chi⁴
same	同樣	tung² yong⁴	t'ung² yang⁴
sample	貨樣	hwor⁴ yong⁴	huo⁴ yang⁴
sanction	核准	haw² joo-n³	ho² chun³
sand	沙土	shah¹ too³	sha¹ t'u³
sanitary	衛生的	way⁴ shung¹ dee¹	wei⁴ shêng¹ ti¹
satin	緞子	dwon⁴ tze³	tuan⁴ tzŭ³
satisfy	滿足	mahn³ dsoo²	man³ tsu²
Saturday	星期六	shing¹ chee² le-oo⁴	hsing¹ ch'i² liu⁴
sauce	醬油	che-ong⁴ yoo²	chiang⁴ yu²
saucepan	蒸鍋	chung² gwor¹	ch'êng² kuo¹
saucer	碟子	de-air² tze³	tieh² tzŭ³
save	救	je-oo⁴	chiu⁴
save (money)	節省	jair² shung³	chieh² shêng³
say	說	shoo-aw¹	shuo¹
scale (fish)	魚鱗	yeu² lin²	yü² lin²

	Chinese	Approximation	Wade
scale (music)	音階	yin¹ jair²	yin¹ chieh²
scale (weighing)	秤	chung⁴	ch'êng⁴
scarf	圍巾	way² jin¹	wei² chin¹
scatter	散開	sahn⁴ ky	san⁴ k'ai¹
scenery	風景	fung¹ jing³	fêng¹ ching³
scholar	學士	shoo-er² shir⁴	hsüeh² shih⁴
school	學校	shoo-er² shaow⁴	hsüeh² hsiao⁴
school (grammar)	小學	she-aow³ shoo-er²	hsiao³ hsüeh²
school (high)	中學	joong¹ shoo-er²	chung¹ hsüeh²
science	科學	cur¹ shoo-er²	k'o¹ hsüeh²
scientific	科學的	cur¹ shoo-er² dee¹	k'o¹ hsüeh² ti¹
scissors	剪刀	jen¹ daow¹	chien¹ tao¹
scold	罵	mah⁴	ma⁴
scream	大叫	dah⁴ je-aow⁴	ta⁴ chiao⁴
screen	屏風	ping² fung¹	p'ing² fêng¹
scrub	洗刷	she³ shwah¹	hsi³ shua¹
scrupulous	謹慎	jin³ shun⁴	chin³ shên⁴
sea	海	hy³	hai³
sea-sickness	暈船	yew-n⁴ chwon²	yün⁴ ch'uan²
seal	密封	mee⁴ fung¹	mi⁴ fêng¹
search	尋察	shew-n² chah²	hsün² ch'a²

	Chinese		Approximation	Wade
season	時	季	shir^2 jee^4	shih^2 chi^4
seat	坐	位	dsaw^4 way^4	tso^4 wei^4
second (time)	一	秒	ee^1 mee-aow^3	i^1 miao^3
second (ordinal)	第	二	dee^4 er^4	ti^4 êrh^4
secret	秘	密	bee^4 mee^4	pi^4 mi^4
sect	派	會	py^4; whay^4	p'ai^4; hui^4
section	節	段	jair^2; dwan^4	chieh^2; tuan^4
secure	穩	固	wun^3 goo^4	wên^3 ku^4
see	看	見	kahn^4 jen^4	k'an^4 chien^4
seed	種	子	joong^3 tze^3	chung^3 tzŭ^3
seek	尋	求	shew-n^2 che-oo^2	hsün^2 ch'iu^2
seem	好	像	haow^4 she-ong^4	hao^4 hsiang^4
seize	捕		boo^3	pu^3
seldom	少	有	shaow^3 yoo^3	shao^3 yu^3
select	選	擇	shew-en^3 dseh^2	hsüan^3 tsê^2
self	自	己	tze^4 jee^3	tsŭ^4 chi^3
self-confident	自	負	tze^4 foo^4	tsŭ^4 fu^4
selfish	自	私	tze^4 sze^1	tsŭ^4 ssŭ
sell	賣		my^4	mai^4
semester	學	期	shoo-er^2 chee^2	hsüeh^2 ch'i^2
send	送	寄	soong^4; jee^4	sung^4; chi^4

	Chinese	Approximation	Wade
senior	年長子	ne-en² chong²	nien² ch'ang²
sentence	句子	jeu⁴ tze³	chü⁴ tzŭ³
sentiment	情	ching²	ch'ing²
sentry	哨兵	shaow⁴ bing¹	shao⁴ ping¹
separate	分別	fun¹ be-air²	fên¹ pieh²
September	九月	jee-oo³ yew-eh⁴	chiu³ yüeh⁴
serious	嚴重	yen² joong⁴	yen² chung⁴
sermon	講道	je-ong¹ daow⁴	chiang¹ tao⁴
servant	傭人	yoong¹ run²	yung¹ jên²
service	服務	foo² woo⁴	fu² wu⁴
settle	安置	ahn¹ jir⁴	an¹ chih⁴
settlement	租界	dsoo¹ jair⁴	tsu¹ chieh⁴
sever	分離	fun¹ lee²	fên¹ li²
several	幾個	jee¹ gur⁴	chi¹ ko⁴
sew	縫	fung²	fêng²
sex	性	shing⁴	hsing⁴
shabby	襤褸	jen⁴ law⁴	chien⁴ lo⁴
shadow	影子	ying³ tze³	ying³ tzŭ³
shake	搖動	yaow² doong⁴	yao² tung⁴
shallow	淺	che-en³	ch'ien³
shame	知恥	jir¹ chir²	chih¹ ch'ih²

	Chinese	Approximation	Wade
shameful	可恥的	cur³ chir² dee¹	k'o³ ch'ih² ti¹
shape (n)	形狀	shing² jwong⁴	hsing² chuang⁴
share (n)	一部份	ee¹ boo⁴ fun¹	i¹ pu⁴ fên¹
share (v)	共享	goong⁴ she-ong³	kung⁴ hsiang³
sharp	尖	jen¹	chien¹
shave	刮臉	kwah¹ le-en³	kua¹ lien³
she	她	tah¹	t'a¹
sheep	羊	yahng²	yang²
sheet (cloth)	單被	dahn¹ bay⁴	tan¹ pei⁴
sheet (paper)	一張紙	ee¹ jong¹ jir³	i¹ chang¹ chih³
shelf	架子	jar⁴ tze³	chia⁴ tzǔ³
shell (artil.)	子彈	tze³ dahn⁴	tzǔ³ tan⁴
shell (musk)	殼	cur¹	k'o¹
shiny	明亮	ming² le-ong⁴	ming² liang⁴
ship (n)	船	chwon²	ch'uan²
ship (cargo)	裝運	jwong¹ yew-n⁴	chuang¹ yün⁴
shipping office	船公司	chwon² goong¹ sze¹	ch'uan² kung¹ ssǔ¹
shirt	襯衫	chun⁴ shahn¹	ch'ên⁴ shan¹
shiver	發料	fah¹ doe³	fa¹ tou³
shoe	鞋子	she-eh¹ tze³	hsieh² tzǔ³
shoot	射	sheh²	shê²

	Chinese	Approximation	Wade
shop	店舖	de-en⁴poo¹	tien⁴p'u¹
shopkeeper	店主	de-en⁴joo³	tien⁴chu³
shore	岸	ahn⁴	an⁴
short	短	dwon³	tuan³
short-cut	短路	dwon³loo⁴	tuan³lu⁴
should	應該	ying¹guy¹	ying¹kai¹
shoulder	肩	jen¹	chien¹
show	指明	jir³ming²	chih³ming²
shower	下雨	shah⁴yeu³	hsia⁴yü³
shut	關	gwan¹	kuan¹
shy	怕羞	pah⁴shee-oo¹	p'a⁴hsiu¹
sick	疾病	jee¹bing⁴	chi¹ping⁴
side	邊	be-en¹	pien¹
sigh	嘆息	tahn⁴she²	t'an⁴hsi²
sight	視力	shir⁴lee⁴	shih⁴li⁴
sign (n)	記號	jee⁴haow⁴	chi⁴hao⁴
sign (v)	簽名	chen¹ming²	ch'ien¹ming²
signature	簽名	chen¹ming²	ch'ien¹ming²
silence	靜默	jing⁴maw⁴	ching⁴mo⁴
silk	絲	sze¹	ssǔ¹
silly	愚笨	yeu²bun⁴	yü²pên⁴

	Chinese	Approximation	Wade
silver	銀	yin²	yin²
similar	相像	shee-ong¹ shee-ong⁴	hsiang¹ hsiang⁴
simmer	慢煮	mahn⁴ joo¹	man⁴ chu¹
simple	簡單	jen³ dahn¹	chien³ tan¹
simultaneous	同時	toong² shir²	t'ung² shih²
sin	罪惡	dsoo-ee⁴ aw⁴	tsui⁴ o⁴
since	既自從	jee⁴; tze⁴ tsoong²	chi⁴; tzŭ⁴ ts'ung²
sincere	誠真	chung²; jun¹	chêng²; chên¹
sinews	筋力	jin¹ lee⁴	chin¹ li⁴
sing	唱	chong⁴	ch'ang⁴
singer	唱歌的	chong⁴ gur¹ dee¹	ch'ang⁴ ko¹ ti¹
single	單獨	dahn¹ doo²	tan¹ tu²
sink	沈	chun²	ch'ên²
sinner	犯罪者	fahn⁴ dsoo-ee⁴ jaw³	fan⁴ tsui⁴ chê³
sister (elder)	姐姐	jair³ jair³	chieh³ chieh³
sister (younger)	妹妹	may⁴ may⁴	mei⁴ mei⁴
sister-in-law	嫂子弟婦	saow³ tze¹ dee⁴ foo¹	sao³ tzŭ¹ ti⁴ fu¹
sisters	姐妹	jair³ may⁴	chieh³ mei⁴
sit	坐	dsaw⁴	tso⁴
size	大小	dah⁴ she-aow³	ta⁴ hsiao³
skates	滑冰鞋	whah² bing¹ she-eh²	hua² ping¹ hsieh²

	Chinese	Approximation	Wade
sketch	寫畫	she-eh^3; whah^4	hsieh^3; hua^4
skill	機巧	jee^1 che-aow^3	chi^1 ch'iao^3
skin	皮膚	pee^2 foo^1	p'i^2 fu^1
skirt	裙	chew-n^2	ch'ün^2
sky	天空	te-en^1 koong^1	t'ien^1 k'ung^1
slave	奴僕	nee-u^2 poo^3	nü^2 p'u^3
sleep	睡	shway^4	shui^4
sleeve	袖子	shee-oo^4 tze^3	hsiu^4 tsŭ^3
slender	細長	she^4 chong^2	hsi^4 ch'ang^2
slice	片	pe-en^4	p'ien^4
slight	微小	way^1 she-aow^3	wei^1 hsiao^3
slip	滑	whah^2	hua^2
slipper	拖鞋	taw^1 she-eh^2	t'o^1 hsieh^2
slope	坡	paw^1	p'o^1
slovenly	衣冠不整	ee^1 gwan^1 boo^1 jung^3	i^1 kuan^1 pu^1 chêng^3
slow	慢	mahn^4	man^4
slowly	慢慢的	mahn^{4}mahn^{4}dee^1	man^{4}man^{4}ti^1
small	小	she-aow^3	hsiao^3
small-pox	痘疹	doh^4 jun^3	tou^4 chên^3
smear	塗	too^2	t'u^2
smell (n)	氣味	chee^4 way^4	ch'i^4 wei^4

146

	Chinese	Approximation	Wade
smell (v)	聞	wun²	wên²
smile	笑	she-aow⁴	hsiao⁴
smoke	烟	yen¹	yen¹
smooth	平滑	ping² whah²	p'ing² hua²
snake	蛇	sheh²	shê²
sneeze	打嚔	dah³ tee⁴	ta³ ti⁴
snow (n)	雪	shew-eh³	hsüeh³
snow (v)	下雪	shah⁴ shew-eh³	hsia⁴ hsüeh³
snowflake	雪花	shew-eh³ whah¹	hsüeh³ hua¹
so	所以	saw³ ee³	so³ i³
soak	浸入	chin⁴ roo⁴	ch'in⁴ ju⁴
soap	肥皂	fay² dsaow⁴	fei² tsao⁴
sob	哭	koo¹	k'u¹
society	社會	sheh⁴ whay⁴	shê⁴ hui⁴
sock	襪子	wah⁴ tze³	wa⁴ tzŭ³
sofa	榻	tah⁴	t'a⁴
soft	軟	roo-ahn³	juan³
soldier	兵士	bing¹ shir⁴	ping¹ shih⁴
sole	鞋底	she-eh² dee³	hsieh² ti³
solid	堅硬	jen¹ ying⁴	chien¹ ying⁴
solution (of problem)	解決	jair³ jew-eh²	chieh³ chüeh²

	Chinese	Approximation	Wade
solution (liquid)	溶液	roong' ee⁴	jung' i⁴
some	有些	yoo³ she-eh'	yu³ hsieh'
somebody	某人	moh³ run²	mou³ jên²
sometimes	有時	yoo³ shir²	yu³ shih²
something	有事	yoo³ shir⁴	yu³ shih⁴
somewhere	某處	moh³ choo³	mou³ ch'u³
son	兒子	er² tze³	êrh² tzŭ³
son-in-law	女婿	neu³ sheu⁴	nü³ hsü⁴
song	歌	gur'	ko'
soon	即刻	jee² cur'	chi² k'o'
soot	煤灰	may² whay'	mei² hui'
soothe	安慰	ahn' whay⁴	an' wei⁴
sore	痛	toong⁴	t'ung⁴
sorry	憂愁	yoo' cho²	yu' ch'ou²
sort	分類	fun' lay⁴	fên' lei⁴
soul	靈魂	ling² hoon²	ling² hun²
sound (n)	聲音	shung' yin'	shêng' yin'
sound (v)	測量	tseh⁴ leong²	ts'ê⁴ liang²
soup	湯	tong'	t'ang'
sour	酸	swon'	suan'
source	來源	ly² yew-en²	lai² yüan²

	Chinese	Approximation	Wade
south	南方	nahn² fong¹	nan² fang¹
south-east	東南	doong¹ nahn²	tung¹ nan²
south-west	西南	she¹ nahn²	hsi¹ nan²
souvenir	記念品	jee⁴ ne-en⁴ pin³	chi⁴ nien⁴ p'in³
Soviet	蘇維埃	soo¹ way² ai²	su¹ wei² ai²
sow	播種	baw⁴ joong³	po⁴ chung³
space	空間	koong¹ jen¹	k'ung¹ chien¹
spade	鏟子	chahn³ tze³	ch'an³ tzŭ³
spare	省用	shung³ yong⁴	shêng³ yung⁴
spark	火星	hwor² shing³	huo² hsing³
sparrow	麻雀	mah² che-aow³	ma² ch'iao³
speak	說話	shoo-aw¹ whah¹	shuo¹ hua¹
special	特別	teh⁴ be-air²	t'ê⁴ pieh²
specialist	專家	jwon¹ jar¹	chuan¹ chia¹
specialize	專門	jwon¹ mun²	chuan¹ mên²
species	種類	joong³ lay⁴	chung³ lei⁴
speck	斑點	bahn¹ de-en³	pan¹ tien³
speech	演說	yen³ shoo-aw¹	yen³ shuo¹
spend	費用	fay⁴ yoong⁴	fei⁴ yung⁴
spider	蜘蛛	jir¹ joo¹	chih¹ chu¹
spin	紡織	fong³ jir¹	fang³ chih¹

149

	Chinese	Approximation	Wade
spine	脊骨	jee³ goo³	chi³ ku³
spirit	靈魂	ling² hoo-n²	ling² hun²
spiritual	精神的	jing¹ shun² dee¹	ching¹ shên² ti¹
spit	吐痰	too⁴ dahn²	t'u⁴ tan²
splendid	很好	hun³ haow³	hên³ hao³
spoil	壞	why⁴	huai⁴
spoon	湯匙	tong¹ shir³	t'ang¹ shih³
spot	地方	dee⁴ fong¹	ti⁴ fang¹
spread	流行	le-oo² shing²	liu² hsing²
spread out	鋪開	poo¹ ky¹	p'u¹ k'ai¹
spring (season)	春季	choo-n¹ jee¹	ch'un¹ chi¹
spring (n. metal)	彈簧	dahn⁴ whong³	tan⁴ huang³
spring (v)	跳	te-aow⁴	t'iao⁴
sprinkle	潑水	paw¹ shway³	p'o¹ shui³
spy	偵探	jung¹ tahn¹	chêng¹ t'an¹
squadron	隊	doo-ee⁴	tui⁴
square	方形	fong¹ shing²	fang¹ hsing²
stage	戲臺	she⁴ ty²	hsi⁴ t'ai²
stain	污點	woo¹ de-en³	wu¹ tien³
stale	陳腐	chun² foo³	ch'ên² fu³
stalk	梗	gung³	kêng³

	Chinese	Approximation	Wade
stamp (n)	郵票	yoo^2 pe-aow^4	yu^2 p'iao^4
stamp (v)	標記	pe-aow^1 jee^4	p'iao^1 chi^4
stand	站起	jahn^4 chee^3	chan^4 ch'i^3
star	星	shing^1	hsing^1
start (n)	開始	ky^1 shir^3	k'ai^1 shih^3
start (v)	動身	doong^4 shun^1	tung^4 shên^1
starve	飢餓	jee^1 ur^2	chi^1 ê^2
state	國家	gwor^2 jar^1	kuo^2 chia^1
statesman	政治家	jung^4 jir^4 jar^1	chêng^4 chih^4 chia
station	車站	chair^1 jahn^4	ch'ê^1 chan^4
station-master	站長	jahn^4 jong^2	chan^4 chang^2
statistics	統計	toong^3 jee^4	t'ung^3 chi^4
statue	石像	shir^2 she-ong^4	shih^2 hsiang^4
statute	法令	fah^3 ling^4	fa^3 ling^4
staunch	忠實的	joong^1 shir^2 dee^1	chung^1 shih^2 ti^1
stay	留	lee-oo^2	liu^2
steal	偷	toe^1	t'ou^1
steam (n)	汽	chee^4	ch'i^4
steam (v)	蒸	jung^1	chêng^1
steamer	汽船	chee^4 chwon^2	ch'i^4 ch'uan^2
steam-guage	汽表	chee^4 be-aow^3	ch'i^4 piao^3

	Chinese	Approximation	Wade
steel (n)	鋼	gong[1]	kang[1]
steel (v)	使 強 硬	shir[3] che-ong[2] ying[4]	shih[3] ch'iang[2] ying[4]
step	步	boo[4]	pu[4]
sterilize	消 毒	she-aow[1] doo[2]	hsiao[1] tu[2]
steward	接 待 員	jair[1] dy[4] yew-en[2]	chieh[1] tai[4] yüan[2]
stethescope	聽 胸 器	ting[4] she-oong[1] chee[4]	t'ing[1] hsiung[1] ch'i[4]
stick	手 杖	sho[3] jong[4]	shou[3] chang[4]
stiff	硬	ying[4]	ying[4]
still (yet)	還	whon[2]	huan[2]
still (be)	靜 的	jing[4] dee[1]	ching[4] ti[1]
sting (n)	刺	tze[4]	ts'ŭ[4]
stink	臭 味	cho[4] way[4]	ch'ou[4] wei[4]
stir	動	doong[4]	tung[4]
stocking	長 襪 子	chong[2] wah[4] tze[3]	ch'ang[2] wa[4] tzŭ[3]
stomach	肚 子	doo[4] tze[3]	tu[4] tzŭ[3]
stone	石 頭	shir[2] toe[2]	shih[2] t'ou[2]
stoop	屈 身	cheu[1] shun[1]	ch'ü[1] shên[1]
stop	停 止	ting[2] jir[3]	t'ing[2] chih[3]
store (n)	店 舖	de-en[4] poo[4]	tien[4] p'u[4]
store (v)	囤 積	too-n[4] jee[1]	t'un[4] chi[1]
storm	暴 雨	baow[4] yeu[3]	pao[4] yü[3]

	Chinese	Approximation	Wade
story	故事	goo⁴ shir⁴	ku⁴ shih⁴
stove	火爐	hwor³ loo²	huo³ lu²
straight	正直	jung⁴ jir²	chêng⁴ chih²
strange	奇怪	chee² gwy⁴	ch'i² kuai⁴
stranger	生客	shung¹ cur⁴	shêng¹ k'o⁴
strategy	軍略	jew-n¹ le-aow⁴	chün¹ liao⁴
straw	稻草	daow¹ tsaow³	tao¹ ts'ao³
stream	小河	she-aow³ haw²	hsiao³ ho²
street	街道	jair¹ daow³	chieh¹ tao³
street-car	電車	de-en⁴ chair¹	tien⁴ ch'ê¹
strength	力氣	lee⁴ chee⁴	li⁴ ch'i⁴
stretch	引伸	yin³ shun¹	yin³ shên¹
stretcher	抬架	ty² jar⁴	t'ai² chia⁴
stretcher-bearer	抬架人	ty² jar⁴ run²	t'ai² chia⁴ jên²
strike (v)	打	dah³	ta³
strike (n)	罷工	bah⁴ goong¹	pa⁴ kung¹
strip	一條	ee⁴ te-aow²	i⁴ t'iao²
strive	努力	noo² lee⁴	nu² li⁴
strong	強健,有力	che-ong² jen; yoo³ lee⁴	ch'iang² chien¹; yu³ li⁴
stub	存根	tsoo-n² gun¹	ts'un² kên¹
student	學生	shoo-er² shung¹	hsüeh² shêng¹

153

	Chinese	Approximation	Wade
study (n)	書房	shoo¹ fong² → $shoo^1 fong^2$	shu¹ fang²
study (v)	讀書	doo² shoo¹	tu² shu¹
stumble	跌倒	de-air¹ daow³	tieh¹ tao³
stupendous	偉大	way³ dah⁴	wei³ ta⁴
stupid	笨蠢	bun; choo-n³	pên;⁴ ch'un³
sturdy	結實	jair¹ shir²	chieh¹ shih²
style	文體	wun² tee³	wên² t'i³
subject	題目	tee² moo⁴	t'i² mu⁴
subscribe	募捐	moo⁴ jew-en¹	mu⁴ chüan¹
subscription	捐欵	jew-en¹ kwon³	chüan¹ k'uan³
substance	物體	woo⁴ tee³	wu⁴ t'i³
substitute	代替	dy⁴ tee⁴	tai⁴ t'i⁴
subtle	巧滑	che-aow³ whah²	ch'iao³ hua²
subtract	減除	jen; choo²	chien; ch'u²
suburb	郊外	je-aow¹ wy⁴	chiao¹ wai⁴
success	成功	chung² goong¹	ch'êng² kung¹
successful	成功的	chung² goong¹ dee¹	ch'êng² kung¹ ti¹
such	如此的	roo² tze³ dee¹	ju² tzŭ³ ti¹
suddenly	忽然	hoo¹ rahn²	hu¹ jan²
sue	訴訟	soo⁴ soong⁴	su⁴ sung⁴
suffer	受傷	sho⁴ shong¹	shou⁴ shang¹

	Chinese	Approximation	Wade
sufficient	足够	dsoo² goh⁴	tsu² kou⁴
sugar	糖	tong²	t'ang²
suicide	自殺	tze¹ shah¹	tzŭ¹ sha¹
suitcase	皮包	pee² baow¹	p'i² pao¹
summer	夏季	shah⁴ jee¹	hsia⁴ chi¹
sum up	共結	goong⁴ jair²	kung⁴ chieh²
sun	太陽	ty⁴ yahng²	t'ai⁴ yang²
Sunday	星期日	shing¹ chee² rih⁴	hsing¹ ch'i² jih⁴
sun-dry	曬	shy⁴	shai⁴
sunrise	日出	rih⁴ choo¹	jih⁴ ch'u¹
sunset	日落	rih⁴ law⁴	jih⁴ lo⁴
superficial	淺薄	chen³ baow³	ch'ien³ pao³
superior	高等	gaow¹ dung³	kao¹ têng³
supernatural	神異	shun² ee⁴	shên² i⁴
superstition	迷信	mee² shin⁴	mi² hsin⁴
supper	晚飯	wan³ fahn⁴	wan³ fan⁴
support (n)	補助	boo³ joo⁴	pu³ chu⁴
support (v)	支持	jir¹ chir²	chih¹ ch'ih²
suppose	假定	jar³ ding⁴	chia³ ting⁴
sure	一定	ee² ding⁴	i² ting⁴
surface	面上	me-en⁴ shong⁴	mien⁴ shang⁴

	Chinese	Approximation	Wade
surgeon	外科醫生	wy⁴ cur' ee' shung'	wai⁴ k'o' i' shêng'
surname	姓	shing⁴	hsing⁴
surplus	敷餘	foo⁴ yeu²	fu⁴ yü²
surprising	奇怪	chee² gwy⁴	ch'i² kuai⁴
surrender	投降	toe² she-ong²	t'ou² hsiang²
surround	包圍	baow' way²	pao' wei²
suspect	疑惑	ee² hwor⁴	i² huo⁴
suspend	懸停止	shew-en; ting² jir³	hsüan; t'ing² chih³
suspicious	多疑	daw' ee²	to' i²
swallow (n)	燕子	yen⁴ tze³	yen⁴ tzŭ³
swallow (v)	吞下	too-n' shah⁴	t'un' hsia⁴
sway	搖	yaow²	yao²
sweat	汗	hahn²	han²
sweat shirt	汗衫	hahn² shahn'	han² shan'
sweep	掃	saow³	sao³
sweet	甜甘	te-en; gahn'	t'ien; kan'
Sweden	瑞典國	roo-ee⁴ de-en³ gwor	jui⁴ tien³ kuo²
sweetheart	情人	ching run²	ch'ing² jên²
swift	快	kwy⁴	k'uai⁴
swim	泅水	foo⁴ shway³	fu⁴ shui³
swing	打秋千	dah³ joo' chen'	ta³ chu' ch'ien'

	Chinese	Approximation	Wade
sword	劍	jen⁴	chien⁴
sympathy	同情心	toong² ching² shin¹	t'ung² ch'ing² hsin¹
system	系統	she⁴ toong³	hsi⁴ t'ung³

T

	Chinese	Approximation	Wade
table	棹子	jaw¹ tze³	cho¹ tzŭ³
tablet	牌	py²	p'ai²
tactics	戰術	jahn⁴ shoo⁴	chan⁴ shu⁴
tail	尾巴	way³ bah¹	wei³ pa¹
tailor	裁縫	tsy² fung²	ts'ai² fêng²
take	拿取	nah; jeu⁴	na; chü⁴
take (away)	拿走	nah² dsoh³	na² tsou³
take care of	當心	dong¹ shin¹	tang¹ hsin¹
talent	才能	tsy² nung²	ts'ai² nêng²
talk (n)	話	whah⁴	hua⁴
talk (v)	説話	shoo-aw¹ whah⁴	shuo¹ hua⁴
tall	高	gaow¹	kao¹
tame	養馴	yong³ shew-n²	yang³ hsün²
Taoism	道教	daow⁴ je-aow⁴	tao⁴ chiao⁴
tardy	遲	chir²	ch'ih²
Tartar	韃子	dah² tze³	ta² tzŭ³
task	工作	goong¹ dsaw⁴	kung¹ tso⁴

	Chinese	Approximation	Wade
taste (n)	滋味	tze² way⁴	tzŭ² wei⁴
taste (v)	嘗味	chong² way⁴	ch'ang² wei⁴
tax (n)	稅	shway⁴	shui⁴
tax (v)	正課	jung¹ cur⁴	chêng¹ k'o⁴
tea	茶葉	chah² yair⁴	ch'a² yeh⁴
tea-pot	茶壺	chah² hoo²	ch'a² hu²
teach	教	je-aow¹	chiao¹
teacher	先生	shen¹ shung¹	hsien¹ shêng¹
tear (v)	斯破	sze¹ paw⁴	ssŭ¹ p'o⁴
tears	眼淚	yen³ lay⁴	yen³ lei⁴
teeth	牙齒	yah² chir³	ya² ch'ih³
telegram	電報	de-en⁴ baow⁴	tien⁴ pao⁴
telephone (n)	電話	de-en⁴ whah⁴	tien⁴ hua⁴
telephone (v)	打電話	dah³ de-en⁴ whah⁴	ta³ tien⁴ hua⁴
telephone book	電話本子	de-en⁴ whah⁴ bun tze³	tien⁴ hua⁴ pên³ tzŭ³
telephone exchange	電話公司	de-en⁴ whah⁴ goong¹ sze¹	tien⁴ hua⁴ kung¹ ssŭ¹
telephone number	電話號數	de-en⁴ whah⁴ haow⁴ shoo⁴	tien⁴ hua⁴ hao⁴ shu⁴
telescope	望遠鏡	wong⁴ yew-en³ jing³	wang⁴ yüan³ ching³
tell	告訴	gaow⁴ soo⁴	kao⁴ su⁴
temper	脾氣	pee² chee⁴	p'i² ch'i⁴
temperature	溫度	wun¹ doo⁴	wên¹ tu⁴

	Chinese	Approximation	Wade
Thursday	星期四	shing¹ chee² sze⁴	hsing¹ ch'i² ssŭ⁴
ticket	票	pe-aow⁴	p'iao⁴
tide	潮水	chaow² shway³	ch'ao² shui³
tidy	乾淨	gahn¹ jing⁴	kan¹ ching⁴
tie (n)	領結	ling³ jair²	ling³ chieh²
tie (v)	拴	shwon¹	shuan¹
tiger	老虎	laow² hoo³	lao² hu³
tight	緊.	jin³	chin³
till	及至	jee² jir⁴	chi² chih⁴
time	時候	shir² hoh²	shih² hou²
timely	合時	haw² shir²	ho² shih²
time-table	時刻表	shir² cur' be-aow³	Shih² k'o' piao³
tin	錫	she²	hsi²
tip (gratuity)	賞錢	shong³ chen²	shang³ ch'ien²
title	名稱	ming² chung¹	ming² chêng¹
tobacco	煙	yen¹	yen¹
today	今天	jin¹ te-en¹	chin¹ t'ien¹
toe	腳指	je-aow³ jir²	chiao³ chih²
together	一同	ee¹ toong²	i¹ t'ung²
toil (n)	勞苦	laow² koo³	lao² k'u³
toil (v)	勞力	laow² lee⁴	lao² li⁴

161

	Chinese	Approximation	Wade
tolerate	容忍	roong² run³	jung² jên³
tomato	西紅柿	she¹ hoong² shir⁴	hsi¹ hung² shih⁴
tombstone	墓碑	moo⁴ bay¹	mu⁴ pei¹
tomorrow	明天	ming² te-en¹	ming² t'ien¹
ton	噸	doo-n⁴	tun⁴
tone	聲音	shung¹ yin¹	shêng¹ yin¹
tongue	舌頭	sheh² toh²	shê² t'ou²
tonight	今晚	jin¹ wan³	chin¹ wan³
too (too much)	太過	ty⁴ gwor⁴	t'ai⁴ kuo⁴
too (as well)	也	yair³	yeh³
tool	工具	goong¹ jeu⁴	kung¹ chü⁴
tooth	牙	yah²	ya²
tooth-ache	牙痛	yah² toong⁴	ya² t'ung⁴
tooth-brush	牙刷	yah² shwah¹	ya² shua¹
tooth-powder	牙粉	yah² fun³	ya² fên³
top	上頭	shong⁴ toh²	shang⁴ t'ou²
topple	倒	daow³	tao³
torpedo (n)	水雷	shway² lay²	shui² lei²
total	總數	dsoong⁴ shoo⁴	tsung⁴ shu⁴
touch	覺	jeweh²	chüeh²
tough	結實	jair¹ shir²	chieh¹ shih²

	Chinese	Approximation	Wade
towards	响	she-ong⁴	hsiang⁴
towel	手巾	sho³ jin¹	shou³ chin¹
tower	手樓	loh²	lou²
town	城市	chung² shir⁴	ch'êng² shih⁴
toys	玩物	wan⁴ woo⁴	wan⁴ wu⁴
track	踪跡	dsoong¹ jee⁴	tsung¹ chi⁴
trade (n)	商業	shong¹ yair⁴	shang¹ yeh⁴
trade (v)	買賣	my³ my⁴	mai³ mai⁴
trademark	商標	shong¹ be-aow¹	shang¹ piao¹
train	火車	hwor³ chair¹	huo³ ch'ê¹
transact	幹辨	gahn⁴ bahn⁴	kan⁴ pan⁴
transaction	交易	je-aow¹ ee⁴	chiao¹ i⁴
transfer (n)	調用	deaow⁴ yoong⁴	tiao⁴ yung⁴
transfer (v)	受授	sho⁴ sho⁴	shou⁴ shou⁴
transform	變化	be-en⁴ whah⁴	pien⁴ hua⁴
transgress	犯法	fahn⁴ fah⁴	fan⁴ fa⁴
translate	翻譯	fahn¹ ee⁴	fan¹ i⁴
transparent	透明	toh⁴ ming²	t'ou⁴ ming²
transport	轉運	jwon⁴ yew-n⁴	chuan⁴ yün⁴
travel	旅行	leu³ shing²	lü³ hsing²
traveller	旅客	leu³ cur⁴	lü³ k'o⁴

163

	Chinese	Approximation	Wade
treasure (n)	藏寶	tsong⁴	ts'ang⁴
treasure (v)	寶貝	baow³ bay⁴	pao³ pei⁴
treat	待遇	dy⁴ yeu⁴	tai⁴ yü⁴
treaty	條約	te-aow² yew-eh¹	t'iao² yüeh¹
tree	樹	shoo⁴	shu⁴
triangle	三角	sahn¹ jaow³	san¹ chiao³
troops	軍隊	jew-n¹ doo-ee⁴	chün¹ tui⁴
trouble	煩	fahn²	fan²
troublesome	費事	fay⁴ shir⁴	fei⁴ shih⁴
trousers	褲子	koo⁴ tze³	k'u⁴ tzǔ³
truck	貨車	hwor⁴ chair¹	huo⁴ ch'ê¹
true	真	jun¹	chên¹
truly	誠然	jung² rahn²	chêng² jan²
trunk (box)	大箱	dah⁴ she-ong¹	ta⁴ hsiang¹
trunk (body)	身軀	shun¹ choo¹	shên¹ ch'u¹
trust (n)	信用	shin⁴ yoong⁴	hsin⁴ yung⁴
trust (v)	相信	she-ong¹ shin⁴	hsiang¹ hsin⁴
truth	真理	jun¹ lee³	chên¹ li³
try	試	shir⁴	shih⁴
tub	木桶	moo⁴ toong³	mu⁴ t'ung³
tuberculosis	肺癆	fay⁴ laow²	fei⁴ lao²

	Chinese	Approximation	Wade
Tuesday	星期二	shing¹ chee² er⁴	hsing¹ ch'i² êrh⁴
tune	調	de-aow⁴	tiao⁴
tunnel	隧道	sway⁴ daow⁴	sui⁴ tao⁴
turkey	火鷄	hwor³ jee¹	huo³ chi¹
turn	轉翻	jwon;⁴ fahn¹	chuan;⁴ fan¹
turn into	變成	be-en⁴ chung²	pien⁴ ch'êng²
twice	兩次	le-ong³ tze⁴	liang³ tz'ŭ⁴
twilight	黃昏	whong² hoo-n¹	huang² hun¹
twin	雙生	shwong⁴ shung¹	shuang⁴ shêng¹
twine	麻線	mah² she-en⁴	ma² hsien⁴
twist	扭	nee-u³	niu³
two	兩個二	le-ong³ cur;⁴ er⁴	liang³ ko;⁴ êrh⁴
typewriter	打字機	dah³ tze⁴ jee¹	ta³ tzŭ⁴ chi¹
type (kind)	種樣	joong;³ yong⁴	chung; yang⁴
typist	打字員	dah³ tze⁴ yew-en²	ta³ tzŭ⁴ yüan²
U			
ugly	醜	choh³	ch'ou³
umbrella	雨傘	yew³ sahn³	yü³ san³
unanimous	齊心	chee² shin¹	ch'i² hsin¹
unavoidable	不能免	boo¹ nung² me-en³	pu¹ nêng² mien³
uncle	叔伯	shoo;³ baw⁴	shu;³ po⁴

	Chinese	Approximation	Wade
uncomfortable	不舒服	boo¹ shoo¹ foo²	pu¹ shu¹ fu²
under	底下	dee³ shah⁴	ti³ hsia⁴
understand	懂	doong³	tung³
understanding	領會	ling³ whay⁴	ling³ hui⁴
uneasy	不安	shin¹ boo⁴ahn¹	hsin¹ pu⁴an¹
unequal	不平等	boo¹ ping² dung³	pu¹ p'ing² têng³
unexpected	意外	ee⁴ wy⁴	i⁴ wai⁴
unfortunate	不幸	boo¹ shing⁴	pu¹ hsing⁴
unhappy	不高興	boo¹ gaow¹ shing⁴	pu¹ kao¹ hsing
uniform (military)	軍服	jew-n¹ foo²	chün¹ fu²
uniform (adj)	均勻	jew-n¹ yew-n¹	chün¹ yün¹
unify	統一	toong³ ee¹	t'ung³ i¹
unimportant	不重要	boo¹ jung⁴ yaow⁴	pu¹ chung⁴ yao⁴
union	聯合	le-en² haw²	lien² ho²
unite	合併	haw² ping⁴	ho² ping⁴
united	同心合一	toong² shin¹ haw² ee¹	t'ung² hsin¹ ho² i¹
universal	普偏的	poo³ be-en⁴ dee¹	p'u³ pien⁴ ti¹
universe	宇宙	yeu³ joh⁴	yü³ chou⁴
University	大學	dah⁴ shoo-er²	ta⁴ hsüeh²
unjust	不公正	boo¹ goong¹ jung⁴	pu¹ kung¹ chêng⁴
unkind	不盡情	boo¹ jin⁴ ching²	pu¹ chin⁴ ch'ing²

	Chinese		Approximation	Wade
unripe	不	熟	boo¹ shoo²	pu¹ shu²
unskilled	外	行	wy⁴ hong²	wai⁴ hang²
unusual	非	常	fay¹ chong²	fei¹ ch'ang²
unwell	不	適	boo¹ shir⁴	pu¹ shih⁴
up	上		shong⁴	shang⁴
upon	上	面	shong⁴ me-en⁴	shang⁴ mien⁴
upright	直		jir²	chih²
upset	顛	覆	de-en¹ foo⁴	tien¹ fu⁴
upstairs	樓	上	loh² shong¹	lou² shang¹
urgent	緊	急	jin³ jee²	chin³ chi²
urinate	小	便	she-aow³ be-en⁴	hsiao³ pien⁴
us	我	們	woh³ men²	wo³ mên²
U.S.A.	美	國	may³ gwor²	mei³ kuo²
use	用	使	yoong⁴; shir³	yung⁴; shih³
useful	有	用	yoo³ yoong⁴	yu³ yung⁴
useless	無	用	woo² yoong⁴	wu² yung⁴
U.S.S.R.	蘇	俄	soo¹ oh²	su¹ ô²
usually	照	常	jaow¹ chong²	chao¹ ch'ang²
usurp	篡	位	tswon⁴ daw²	ts'uan⁴ to²
utensil	傢	伙	jar² hwor²	chia² huo²
utilize	利	用	lee⁴ yoong⁴	li⁴ yung⁴

	Chinese	Approximation	Wade
utmost	極端	jee² dwan¹	chi² tuan¹
utter	發言	fah¹ yen²	fa¹ yen²
V			
vacate	搬出	bahn¹ choo¹	pan¹ ch'u¹
vacation	假期	jar⁴ chee²	chia⁴ ch'i²
vaccinate	種痘	joong³ doh⁴	chung³ tou⁴
vague	不確定	boo¹ chee-aw⁴ ding⁴	pu¹ ch'io⁴ ting⁴
vain	不虛	sheu¹	hsü¹
valley	山谷	shahn¹ koo³	shan¹ k'u³
valuable	貴重的	gway⁴ joong⁴ dee⁴	kuei⁴ chung⁴ ti⁴
value (n)	價值	jar⁴ jir²	chia⁴ chih²
value (v)	估價	goo¹ jar⁴	ku¹ chia⁴
vanity	虛榮	sheu¹ roong²	hsü¹ jung²
vapour	氣	chee⁴	ch'i⁴
variation	變形	be-en⁴ shing²	pien⁴ hsing²
variety	種類	joong³ lay⁴	chung³ lei⁴
various	好幾種	haow³ jee¹ joong³	hao³ chi¹ chung³
vast	浩大	haow⁴ dah⁴	hao⁴ ta⁴
vegetable	蔬菜	soo⁴ tsy⁴	su⁴ ts'ai⁴
vegetation	草木	tsaow³ moo⁴	ts'ao³ mu⁴
veins	脈	maw⁴	mo⁴

	Chinese	Approximation	Wade
venerable	可敬	cur³ jing⁴	k'o³ ching⁴
venetian blinds	百頁窗	by³ yair¹ chwong¹	pai³ yeh¹ ch'uang¹
ventilator	通氣具	toong¹ chee⁴ jeu⁴	tung¹ ch'i⁴ chü⁴
verb	動詞	doong⁴ tze⁴	tung⁴ tzǔ⁴
vernacular	土話	too³ whah⁴	t'u³ hua⁴
versatility	多才	daw¹ tsy²	to¹ t'sai²
verse	詩	shir¹	shih¹
very	很 甚	hun;³ shun²	hên;³ shên²
veterinary-surgeon	獸醫	sho⁴ ee¹	shou⁴ i¹
vexation	煩膩	fahn² naow³	fan² nao³
vice	惡習	aw⁴ she²	ô⁴ hsi²
vicious	惡劣	aw⁴ le-air⁴	ô⁴ lieh⁴
victorious	得勝	deh² shung⁴	tê² shêng⁴
victory	勝利	shung⁴ lee⁴	shêng⁴ li⁴
view	眼界	yen³ jair³	yen³ chieh³
village	鄉村	she-ong¹ tsoo-n¹	hsiang¹ ts'un¹
vinegar	醋	tsoo⁴	ts'u⁴
violent	兇暴	she-oong¹ baow⁴	hsiung¹ pao⁴
violin	胡琴	hoo¹ chin²	hu¹ ch'in²
virtue	德行	deh² shing²	tê² hsing²
visa	簽証	chen¹ jung⁴	ch'ien¹ chêng⁴

	Chinese	Approximation	Wade
vision	眼力	yen^3 lee^4	yen^3 li^4
visit	拜訪	by^4 fong^3	pai^4 fang^3
voice	聲音	shung^1 yin^1	shêng^1 yin^1
volume	書冊	shoo^1 tseh^4	shu^1 t'sê^4
voluntary	自願的	tze^4 yew-en^4 dee^1	tzŭ^4 yüan^4 ti^1
volunteer (n)	義兵	ee^4 bing^1	i^4 ping^1
vote	投票	toh^2 pe-aow^4	t'ou^2 p'iao^4
vowel	母音	moo^3 yin^1	mu^3 yin^1
voyage	航海	hong^2 hy^3	hang^2 hai^3
voyager	航客	hong^2 cur^4	hang^2 k'o^4
vulgar	卑下	bay^1 shah^4	pei^1 hsia^4
W			
wade	涉水	sheh^4 shway^3	shê^4 shui^3
wages	工錢	goong^1 chen^2	kung^1 ch'ien^2
wagon	大車	dah^4 chair^1	ta^4 ch'ê^1
waist	腰	yaow^1	yao^1
wait	等候	dung^3 hoh^4	têng^3 hou^4
waiter	茶房	chah^2 fong^2	ch'a^2 fang^2
waiting-room	待客廳	dy^4 cur^4 ting^1	tai^4 k'o^4 t'ing^1
wake	醒	shing^3	hsing^3
walk	行走	shing^2 dsoh^3	hsing^2 tsou^3

	Chinese	Approximation	Wade
wall	墙	che-ong³	ch'iang²
wander	閒遊	she-en yoo²	hsien yu²
want	要	yaow⁴	yao⁴
war	戰爭	jahn⁴ jung¹	chan⁴ chêng¹
warehouse	棧房	jahn⁴ fong²	chan⁴ fang²
warm	溫暖	wun¹ nwon³	wên¹ nuan³
wash	洗	she³	hsi³
wasp	黃蜂	wong² fung¹	huang² fêng¹
waste (n)	廢物	fay⁴ woo⁴	fei⁴ wu⁴
waste (v)	浪廢	lahng⁴ fay⁴	lang⁴ fei⁴
watch (n)	錶	be-aow³	piao³
watch (v)	待看	dy¹ kahn⁴	tai¹ k'an⁴
water	水	shway³	shui³
water-bottle	水瓶	shway³ ping²	shui³ p'ing²
wave (n)	波浪	baw¹ lahng⁴	po¹ lang⁴
wave (v)	搖手	yaow² sho³	yao² shou³
wax	蠟	lah⁴	la⁴
way	道路	daow⁴ loo⁴	tao⁴ lu⁴
we	我們	woh³ men²	wo³ mên²

	Chinese	Approximation	Wade
weak	弱	raw[4]	jô[4]
wealth	財產	tsy[2] chahn[3]	ts'ai[2] ch'an[3]
wealthy	富有	foo[1] yoo[3]	fu[1] yu[3]
weapon	兵器	bing[1] chee[4]	ping[1] ch'i[4]
wear	戴穿	dy; [4] chwon[1]	tai; [4] ch'uan[1]
weather	天氣	te-en[1] chee[4]	t'ien[1] ch'i[4]
wedding	婚姻	hoo-n[1] yin[1]	hun[1] yin[1]
Wednesday	星期三	shing[1] chee[2] sahn[1]	hsing[1] ch'i[2] san[1]
week	星期	shing[1] chee[2]	hsing[1] ch'i[2]
weep	哭	koo[1]	k'u[1]
weigh	秤	chung[1]	ch'êng[1]
weight	分量	fun le-ong[4]	fên liang[4]
welcome	歡迎	whon[1] ying[2]	huan[1] ying[2]
well (n)	井	jing[3]	ching[3]
west	西	she[1]	hsi[1]
whale	鯨魚	jing[1] yeu[1]	ching[1] yü[1]
wharf	碼頭	mah[3] toh[2]	ma[3] t'ou[2]
wet	濕	shir[1]	shih[1]
what	甚麼	shuh[2] maw[1]	shên[2] mo[1]
wheat	小麥	she-aow[3] my[4]	hsiao[3] mai[4]
wheel	輪子	loo-n[2] tze[3]	lun[2] tzŭ[3]

	Chinese	Approximation	Wade
when	何時 裏	haw² shir²	ho² shih²
where	那裏	nah³ lee³	na³ li³
which	那個	nah³ gur⁴	na³ ko⁴
whip	鞭子	be-en¹ tze³	pien¹ tzŭ³
whisper (n)	耳語	er³ yeu³	êrh³ yü³
whistle	吹哨	chway¹ shaow⁴	ch'ui¹ shao⁴
white	白	by²	pai²
who	誰	shoo-ee²	shui²
whole	整個	jung³ gur⁴	chêng³ ko⁴
wholesale	批發	pee¹ fah¹	p'i¹ fa¹
whose	誰的	shoo-ee² dee¹	shui² ti¹
why	何以	haw² ee³	ho² i³
wicked	惡	aw⁴	ô⁴
wickedness	惡性	aw⁴ shing⁴	ô⁴ hsing⁴
wide	寬廣	kwon¹ gwong³	k'uan¹ kuang³
widow	寡婦	gwah³ foo⁴	kua³ fu⁴
widower	鰥夫	gwon¹ foo¹	kuan¹ fu¹
wife	婦妻	foo;⁴ chee¹	fu;⁴ ch'i¹
wild	野	yair³	yeh³
will (n)	意志	ee⁴ jir⁴	i⁴ chih⁴
willing	願意	yew-en⁴ ee⁴	yüan⁴ i⁴

English	Chinese	Approximation	Wade
win	贏,勝	ying²; shung⁴	ying²; shêng⁴
wind (n)	風	fung¹	fêng¹
wind (v)	繞	raow⁴	jao⁴
window	窗戶	chwong¹ hoo⁴	ch'uang¹ hu⁴
wine	酒	jee-oo³	chiu³
wing	翅膀	chir⁴ bong³	ch'ih⁴ pang³
winter	冬天	doong¹ te-en¹	tung¹ t'ien¹
wipe	擦	tsah¹	ts'a¹
wisdom	智慧	jir⁴ whay⁴	chih⁴ hui⁴
wise	聰明	tsoong¹ ming²	ts'ung¹ ming²
wish (n)	希望	she⁴ wong⁴	hsi⁴ wang⁴
wish (v)	願意	yèw-en⁴ ee⁴	yüan⁴ i⁴
with	和,同	haw²; toong²	ho²; t'ung²
within	裏頭,內	lee³ toh²; nay⁴	li³ t'ou²; nei⁴
without	外頭,無	wy⁴ toh²; woo²	wai⁴ t'ou²; wu²
wolf	狼	lahng²	lang²
woman	女人	neu³ run²	nü³ jên²
wood	木料,樹林	moo⁴ le-aow⁴; shoo⁴ lin²	mu⁴ liao⁴; shu⁴ lin²
wool	羊毛	yong² maow²	yang² mao²
words	言詞	yin² tze²	yen² tz'ŭ²
work (n)	工夫	goong¹ foo¹	kung¹ fu¹

	Chinese	Approximation	Wade
work (v)	做工	dsaw⁴ goong¹	tso⁴ kung¹
world	世界	shir⁴ jair⁴	shih⁴ chieh⁴
worm	蟲子	choong¹ tze³	ch'ung² tzŭ³
worry	憂慮	yoo¹ leu⁴	yu¹ lü⁴
worship	拜神	by⁴ shun²	pai⁴ shên²
worst	最下的	dsway⁴ shah⁴ dee¹	tsui⁴ hsia⁴ ti¹
worth	值	jir²	chih²
worthless	不值	boo⁴ jir²	pu⁴ chih²
wound (n)	傷口	shong¹ koh³	shang¹ k'ou³
wound (v)	傷	shong¹	shang¹
wrangle	爭	jung¹	chêng¹
wrap up	打包	dah³ baow¹	ta³ pao¹
wreck	打破	dah³ paw⁴	ta³ p'o⁴
write	寫	she-eh³	hsieh³
writing	字手筆	tze⁴; shoh bee³	tzŭ⁴; shou³ pi³
wrong	錯不對	tsaw⁴; boo² doo-ee⁴	ts'o⁴; pu² tui⁴
Y			
yam	白薯	by² shoo³	pai² shu³
yard	廠碼	chong³; mah³	ch'ang³; ma³
yawn	打哈歲	dah³ hah¹	ta³ ha¹
year	年	ne-en² soo-ee⁴	nien² sui⁴

English	Chinese	Approximation	Wade
yearly	每年	may ne-en^2	mei^3 nien^2
yellow	黃	whong^2	huang^2
yes	是	shir^4	shih^4
yesterday	昨天	dsaw^2 te-en^1	tso^2 t'ien^1
yet	而,仍	er^2; rung^2	êrh^2; jêng^2
yield	讓	rong^4	jang^4
yoke	駕	jar^4	chia^4
you (singular)	你	nee^3	ni^3
you (plural)	你們	nee^3 men^2	ni^3 mên^2
young	少青年	shaow^4; ching^1 ne-en^2	shao^4; ch'ing^1 nien^2
your	你的	nee^3 dee^1	ni^3 ti^1
yourself	你自己	nee^3 tze^4 jee^3	ni^3 tzŭ^4 chi^3
youthful	年輕	ne-en^2 ching^1	nien^2 ch'ing^1

Z

English	Chinese	Approximation	Wade
zenith	絕頂	jew-eh^2 ding^3	chüeh^2 ting^3
zero	零點	ling^2 de-en^3	ling^2 tien^3
zone	地帶	dee^4 dy^4	ti^4 tai^4
zoo	動物園	doong^4 woo^4 yew-en^2	tung^4 wu^4 yüan^2

APPENDIX

The Radicals

1 stroke

1	一	i^1	one	20	勹	pao^1	to wrap up
2	丨	kun^3	a down stroke	21	匕	pi^3	spoon
3	丶	chu^3	a point	22	匚	fang^1	box
4	丿	p'ieh^3	stroke to the left	23	匸	hsi^3	to conceal
5	亅	i^4	a hook	24	十	shih^2	ten
6	乙	chüeh^2	a barb	25	卜	pu^3	to divide

2 strokes

				26	卩	chieh^2	a joint
7	二	êrh^4	two	27	厂	han^4	cliff
8	亠	t'ou^2	above	28	厶	ssŭ^1	selfish
9	人	jên^2	man	29	又	yu^4	also; again
10	儿	jên^2	man				

3 strokes

11	入	ju^4	to enter	30	口	k'ou^3	mouth
12	八	pa^1	eight	31	囗	wei^2	to enclose
13	冂	chiung^3	a limit	32	土	t'u^3	earth
14	冖	mi^4	to cover	33	士	shih^4	scholar
15	冫	ping^1	icicle	34	夂	chih^4	to follow
16	几	chi^1	bench	35	夊	ts'ui^1	to walk slowly
17	凵	k'an^3	receptacle	36	夕	hsi^4	evening
18	刀	tao^1	knife	37	大	ta^4	great
19	力	li^4	strength	38	女	nü^3	woman

39	子	tzǔ[3]	son; a philosopher	4 strokes			
40	宀	mien[2]	a covering	61	心	hsin[1]	heart
41	寸	ts'un[4]	inch	62	戈	ko[1]	spear
42	小	hsiao[3]	small	63	戶	hu[4]	door
43	尢	wang[1]	lame	64	手	shou[3]	hand
44	尸	shih[1]	corpse	65	支	chih[1]	a branch
45	屮	ch'ê[4]	a sprout	66	攴	p'u[1]	to tap
46	山	shan[1]	mountain	67	文	wên[2]	stripes
47	巛	ch'uan[1]	a stream	68	斗	tou[3]	a peck
48	工	kung[1]	labor	69	斤	chin[1]	a pound; axe
49	己	chi[3]	self	70	方	fang[1]	square; then
50	巾	chin[1]	napkin	71	无	wu[2]	negative
51	干	kan[1]	a shield; to concern	72	日	jih[4]	sun; day
52	幺	yao[1]	immature	73	曰	yüeh[1]	to say
53	广	yen[3]	projecting roof	74	月	yüeh[4]	moon; month
54	廴	yin[3]	to move on	75	木	mu[4]	wood; tree
55	廾	kung[3]	hands folded	76	欠	ch'ien[4]	to owe
56	弋	i[4]	a dart	77	止	chih[3]	to stop
57	弓	kung[1]	a bow	78	歹	tai[3]	bad
58	彐	ch'i[4]	pig's head	79	殳	shu[1]	to kill
59	彡	shan[1]	feathers	80	毋	wu[2]	do not
60	彳	ch'ih[4]	a step with left foot	81	比	pi[3]	to compare

#	Character	Romanization	Meaning	#	Character	Romanization	Meaning
82	毛	mao^2	hair	103	疋	p'i^3	a piece of cloth
83	氏	shih^4	family	104	疒	ni^4	disease
84	气	ch'i^4	breath	105	癶	po^4	back to back
85	水	shui^3	water	106	白	pai^2	white
86	火	huo^3	fire	107	皮	p'i^2	skin
87	爪	chao^3	claws	108	皿	min^3	dish
88	父	fu^4	father	109	目	mu^4	eye
89	爻	yao^2	crosswise	110	矛	mou^2	lance
90	爿	ch'iang^2	a contraction of ch'uang a bed	111	矢	shih^3	arrow
91	片	p'ien^4	a slice or slip	112	石	shih^2	stone
92	牙	ya^2	back-teeth	113	示	shih^4	divine
93	牛	niu^2	ox	114	肉	jou^2	footprint
94	犬	ch'üan^3	dog	115	禾	ho^2	growing corn

5 strokes

#	Character	Romanization	Meaning	#	Character	Romanization	Meaning
95	玄	yüan^2	dark	116	穴	hsüeh^4	cave
96	玉	yü^4	jade stone	117	立	li^4	to set up
97	瓜	kua^1	gourd				

6 strokes

#	Character	Romanization	Meaning	#	Character	Romanization	Meaning
98	瓦	wa^3	a tile	118	竹	chu^2	bamboo
99	甘	kan^1	sweet	119	米	mi^3	rice
100	生	shêng^1	to produce	120	糸	ssŭ^1	silk
101	用	yung^4	to use	121	缶	fou^3	earthenware
102	田	t'ien^2	field	122	网	wang^3	a net

123	羊	yang^2	sheep	145	衣	i^1	clothes
124	羽	yü^3	feathers	146	襾	ya^4	to cover
125	老	lao^3	old			**7 strokes**	
126	而	êrh^2	and; but	147	見	chien^4	to see
127	耒	lei^3	plough	148	角	chüeh^2	a horn; an angle
128	耳	êrh^3	ear	149	言	yen^2	words; to speak
129	聿	yü^4	pen	150	谷	ku^3	valley
130	肉	jou^4	flesh	151	豆	tou^4	beans
131	臣	ch'ên^2	a minister	152	豕	shih^4	pig
132	自	tzŭ^4	from; self	153	豸	chai^4	reptile
133	至	chih^4	to go to	154	貝	pei^4	cowry; precious
134	臼	chiu^4	a mortar	155	赤	ch'ih^4	flesh color
135	舌	shê^2	tongue	156	走	tsou^3	to go
136	舛	ch'uan^3	contradictory	157	足	tsu^2	foot; enough
137	舟	chou^1	boat	158	身	shên^1	body
138	艮	kên^4	perverse	159	車	ch'ê^1	cart
139	色	sê^4	color	160	辛	hsin^1	bitter
140	艸	ts'ao^3	grass	161	辰	ch'ên^2	time
141	虍	hu^3	tiger	162	辵	ch'o^4	to walk
142	虫	ch'ung^2	insect	163	邑	i^4	a city
143	血	hsieh^3	blood	164	酉	yu^3	5 to 7 p.m.
144	行	hsing^2	to do; to go	165	釆	pien^4	to distinguish

166	里	li³	a Chinese mile	185	首	shou²	the head
		8 strokes		186	香	hsiang¹	fragrant
167	金	chin¹	gold; metal				
168	長	ch'ang²	long			**10 strokes**	
169	門	mên²	gate; door	187	馬	ma³	horse
170	阜	fou⁴	mound	188	骨	ku³	bone
171	隶	tai⁴	to reach to	189	高	kao¹	high
172	隹	chui¹	short-tailed birds	190	髟	piao¹	long hair
173	雨	yü³	rain	191	鬥	tou⁴	to fight
174	青	ch'ing¹	color of nature green; blue; black	192	鬯	ch'ang⁴	fragrant herbs
175	非	fei¹	not; wrong	193	鬲	li⁴	caldron
				194	鬼	kuei³	spirits of the dead
		9 strokes				**11 strokes**	
176	面	mien⁴	face	195	魚	yü²	fish
177	革	ko²	raw hide	196	鳥	niao³	bird
178	韋	wei²	leather	197	鹵	lu³	salt
179	韭	chiu³	leeks	198	鹿	lu⁴	deer
180	音	yin¹	sound	199	麥	mai⁴	wheat
181	頁	yeh⁴	leaf of a book	200	麻	ma²	hemp
182	風	fêng¹	wind			**12 strokes**	
183	飛	fei¹	to fly	201	黄	huang²	yellow
184	食	shih²	to eat	202	黍	shu³	glutinous millet

203	黑	hei[1]	black
204	黹	chih[2]	embroidery

13 strokes

205	黽	min[3]	frog
206	鼎	ting[3]	tripod
207	鼓	ku[3]	drum
208	鼠	shu[2]	rat

20
14 strokes

209	鼻	pi[3]	nose
210	齊	ch'i[2]	even; equal

15 strokes

211	齒	ch'ih[3]	front-teeth

16 strokes

212	龍	lung[2]	dragon
213	龜	kuei[1]	tortoise

17 strokes

214	龠	yo[4]	flute

The Numeral Adjuncts or Classifiers

個	gur	ko^4	general classifier of persons and things.
位	way	wei^4	classifier of persons.
本	bun	pên^3	books and documents.
件	jen	chien^4	affairs, clothes, documents.
張	jong	chang$^{\prime}$	tables, papers and documents.
塊	kwy	k'uai^4	money and land.
把	bah	pa^3	knives, forks, chairs, fans.
條	te-aow	t'iao^2	streets, fish and long, slender things.
間	jen	chien$^{\prime}$	rooms and houses.
所	saw	so^3	houses.
座	dsaw	tso^3	temples and graves.
口	koh	k'ou^3	words, bells, persons.
頭	toh	t'ou^2	mules, oxen, donkeys.
匹	pee	p'i^3	horses.
疋	pee	p'i^3	bolts of cloth, silk, etc.
扇	shahn	shan^4	doors, windows, screens.
隻	jir	chih$^{\prime}$	oxen, sheep, fowls, limbs, ships.
輛	leong	liang^4	carts and vehicles.
管	gwon	kuan^3	pens, flutes, tubular things.
道	daow	tao^4	streets, rivers, bridges.
顆	cur	k'o$^{\prime}$	trees.

根	gun	kên′	sticks, poles, masts, ropes.
封	fung	fêng′	letters and parcels.
頂	ding	ting³	hats and sedan chairs.
尊	tsoo-n	ts'un′	guns.
枝	jir	chih′	pens and pencils.

The Chinese Numerals

1	一	ee	i'
2	二	er	êrh⁴
3	三	sahn	san'
4	四	sze	ssŭ⁴
5	五	woo	wu³
6	六	le-oo	liu⁴
7	七	chee	ch'i'
8	八	bah	pa'
9	九	je-oo	chiu³
10	十	shir	shih²
12	十二	shir er	shih² êrh⁴
20	二十	er shir	êrh⁴ shih²
35	三十五	sahn shir woo	san' shih² wu³
50	五十	woo shir	wu³ shih²
87	八十七	bah shir chee	pa' shih² ch'i'
99	九十九	je-oo shir je-oo	chiu³ shih² chiu³
100	一百	ee by	i' pai³
1000	一千	ee chen	i' ch'ien'
10,000	一萬	ee wan	i' wan⁴
100,000	十萬	shir wan	shih² wan⁴

100,000	一億	ee ee	i^1 i^4
1,000,000	一百萬	by wan	pai^3 wan^4
1/10	錢	chen	$ch'ien^2$
1/100	分	fun	$fên^1$

The Five Sovereigns	五帝	B.C. 2697-2205
Hsia Dynasty	夏	2205-1766
Shang or Yin Dynasty	商 or 殷	1766-1122
Chou Dynasty	周	1122-255
Ch'in Dynasty	秦	255-206
Han Dynasty	漢	206-A.D. 221
The Three Kingdoms	三國	A.D. 221-265
Wei	魏	
Shu-Han	蜀漢	
Wu	吳	
Tsin Dynasty	晉	265-316
Northern and Southern Empires	南北朝	316-589
Sui Dynasty	隋	589-618
T'ang Dynasty	唐	618-907
Five Dynasty Period (Wu Tai)	五代	907-960
Sung Dynasty	宋	960-1280
Yuan (Mongol) Dynasty	元	1280-1368
Ming Dynasty	明	1368-1644
Ch'ing (Manchu) Dynasty	清	1644-1911
Republic	民國	1911-

Heilungkiang	黑龍江
Kirin	吉林
Liaoning	遼寧
Jehol	熱河
Chahar	察哈爾
Suiyuan	綏遠
Ninghsia	寧夏
Mongolia	蒙古
Sinkiang	新疆
Hopei	河北
Shansi	山西
Shensi	陝西
Kansu	甘肅
Tsinghai	青海
Shantung	山東
Honan	河南
Kiangsu	江蘇
Anhwei	安徽
Hupeh	湖北
Szechuan	四川

190

Sikang	西康
Chekiang	浙江
Fukien	福建
Kiangsi	江西
Hunan	湖南
Kweichow	貴州
Kwangtung	廣東
Kwangsi	廣西
Yunnan	雲南
Tibet	西藏